"This is a first-class primer for anyone who wants to understand what is happening in Israel and Palestine, and what has brought the situation to this point. More than this, Alain Epp Weaver offers an astute and clearly presented discussion that will be useful in classrooms and to anyone committed to peace with justice for all the peoples living in the land."

—MELANIE A DUGUID-MAY
Colgate Rochester Crozer Divinity School

"The thoughtful and compassionate introductory do's and don'ts for discussing the conflict alone are worth the price of admission, but there is much more here for those who want to hear from an often-unheard voice. Jews and Christians engaged in interfaith dialogue should pay special attention."

—SAM BRODY
University of Kansas

"Like an expert tour guide, Alain Epp Weaver's brilliant book provides a clear map through the complex and fraught histories, politics, and theologies of the Palestinian-Israeli conflict. In both accessible and nuanced prose, Epp Weaver introduces readers to the deep Jewish and Palestinian connection to the Land, the emergence of Zionism and Christian Zionism, Palestinian movements, and the perspectives and resilience of Palestinian Christians. His proposal for binationalism and a shared non-possessive mutual belonging is more honest, hopeful, and prophetic than the continued binaries of two-states or competing nationalisms. Read this book!"

—JOSHUA RALSTON
University of Edinburgh

D1479012

"Building on a hopeful and prophetic vision of peaceful transformation of conflict, Epp Weaver offers readers a thoughtful theological reflection on the Palestinian-Israeli conflict. . . . I will recommend this as one of the essential books that travelers to the Holy Land ought to read."

—GORDON MATTIES
Canadian Mennonite University

"*Inhabiting the Land* gives critical attention to the theologies that shape and are shaped by the situation in Palestine-Israel. Epp Weaver has written an introduction that helpfully outlines how these theologies do not sit in isolation, but emerge from the histories of Palestine-Israel and Christian attempts to understand Zionism, the modern State of Israel, and the catastrophe of Palestinian dispossession. Whether you are new to the conversation or not, this is an important read."

—TIMOTHY SEIDEL
Eastern Mennonite University

INHABITING THE LAND

CASCADE COMPANIONS

The Christian theological tradition provides an embarrassment of riches: from Scripture to modern scholarship, we are blessed with a vast and complex theological inheritance. And yet this feast of traditional riches is too frequently inaccessible to the general reader.

The Cascade Companions series addresses the challenge by publishing books that combine academic rigor with broad appeal and readability. They aim to introduce nonspecialist readers to that vital storehouse of authors, documents, themes, histories, arguments, and movements that comprise this heritage with brief yet compelling volumes.

TITLES IN THIS SERIES:

INHABITING THE LAND

*Thinking Theologically about the
Palestinian-Israeli Conflict*

ALAIN EPP WEAVER

 CASCADE *Books* · Eugene, Oregon

INHABITING THE LAND
Thinking Theologically about the Palestinian-Israeli Conflict

Cascade Companions 39

Copyright © 2018 Alain Epp Weaver. All rights reserved. Except for brief quotations in critical publications or reviews, no part of this book may be reproduced in any manner without prior written permission from the publisher. Write: Permissions, Wipf and Stock Publishers, 199 W. 8th Ave., Suite 3, Eugene, OR 97401.

Cascade Books
An Imprint of Wipf and Stock Publishers
199 W. 8th Ave., Suite 3
Eugene, OR 97401

www.wipfandstock.com

PAPERBACK ISBN: 978-1-4982-9430-0
HARDCOVER ISBN: 978-1-4982-9432-4
EBOOK ISBN: 978-1-4982-9431-7

Cataloguing-in-Publication data:

Names: Weaver, Alain Epp, author.

Title: Inhabiting the land : thinking theologically about the Palestinian-Israeli Conflict / Alain Epp Weaver.

Description: Eugene, OR: Cascade Books, 2018 | Cascade Companions 39 | Includes bibliographical references.

Identifiers: ISBN 978-1-4982-9430-0 (paperback) | ISBN 978-1-4982-9432-4 (hardcover) | ISBN 978-1-4982-9431-7 (ebook)

Subjects: LCSH: Arab-Israeli conflict. | Christian Zionism. | Zionism. | National liberation movements—Palestine.| Judaism (Christian theology). |

Classification: DS119.7 .W43 2018 (paperback) | DS119.7 .W43 (ebook)

Manufactured in the U.S.A.   08/29/18

To friends in Zababdeh, Gaza, and Jerusalem,
who inhabit the land and embody sumud

Yaa rabb as-salaam
amtar ʿalayna salaam.
Yaa rabb as-salaam
imlaʾ bilaadina salaam.

O Lord of peace
rain peace upon us.
O Lord of peace
fill our homeland with peace.

—ARABIC CHRISTIAN HYMN
SUNG THROUGHOUT PALESTINE

CONTENTS

ACKNOWLEDGMENTS

THIS BOOK IS DEDICATED to friends in Gaza, Jerusalem, and the West Bank village of Zababdeh, friends who have weathered steadily deteriorating and increasingly grim political realities while maintaining their place in the land with rooted steadfastness (*sumud*). My deep appreciation to Christian Amondson for first suggesting this project and to Charlie Collier and Matthew Wimer for their editorial guidance. Thanks to the Applied Research Institute-Jerusalem and to Frederick Yocum for their work on the maps at the end of this book. Thanks also to Mennonite Central Committee for granting me a study leave during which I completed most of this manuscript. I am immensely grateful to Sam Brody, Krista Johnson Weicksel, Ed Nyce, Tim Seidel, Melanie Duguid-May, and Gordon Matties for their thoughtful input on earlier drafts of this book. Finally, as always, I am deeply indebted to Sonia Weaver, whose critical insights were invaluable and whose searching intellect and unflagging passion took us to Palestine in the first place.

INTRODUCTION

They shall all sit under their own vines
and under their own fig trees,
    and no one shall make them afraid;
    for the mouth of the Lord of hosts has spoken.

—MICAH 4:4

THE PROPHET MICAH PROCLAIMS God's promise of a coming day when God's people will live securely in the land, sitting free from fear under their own vines and fig trees. This prophetic vision offers a word of hope for people uprooted by conflict, hope of a future of landed security. These words of hope from Micah guide this introduction to how to think theologically about one particular conflict—specifically, the Palestinian-Israeli conflict. Theological reflection on that conflict, this book contends, should be carried out in a spirit of hope for a coming day in which Palestinians and Israelis alike will enjoy landed security, with no one to make them afraid. Given the physical barriers that increasingly separate Palestinians and Israelis and the enmity these walls reflect and nurture, this hope may sometimes appear tenuous and even naïve, an unaccountable hope within hopeless circumstances. Yet this hope is grounded in faith in a God who, through Jesus Christ, breaks down dividing walls of hostility, reconciling enemies with one another (Eph 2:10–20).

This book is a specifically Christian examination of how to think theologically about the Israeli-Palestinian conflict. More particularly, this book pays sustained attention to how Palestinian Christians think theologically about the conflict, analyzing how they have encountered and interpreted Zionism, as a multidimensional movement to establish a Jewish state and renew Jewish life in the biblical land of Israel, and assessing their visions for the future. These Palestinian Christian theologies do not, of course, exist in a vacuum, but are part of broader histories and conversations. This book does not presume that the reader has prior knowledge of these broader histories and thus also serves as an introduction to Zionism, the Palestinian national movement, and the conflict between them. The following chapters narrate and assess this wider context, analyzing how Palestinian Christian theologies are embedded within and engage broader Palestinian and Israeli histories as well as wider Christian conversations about how to understand Zionism and the modern State of Israel. Over the course of examining Christian theological interpretations of the Palestinian-Israeli conflict, the book also gives consideration to the varied ways that Jews and Muslims think theologically about the conflict.

This book also does not pretend to be dispassionate. Writing this book emerged from the decade I spent working for a Christian humanitarian organization in different parts of the Occupied Territories—from Zababdeh, a predominantly Christian village in the northern West Bank, to the Gaza Strip, and finally to Jerusalem. This work involved close partnerships with Palestinian churches and with Israeli and Palestinian organizations committed to striving for justice and building peace for all peoples in the land. My family and I became friends with neighbors in Zababdeh, Gaza, and Jerusalem and in the process saw how their lives were shaped by dispossession and military occupation. We also became friends with Israeli Jews working for a just peace in Israel and Palestine. My analysis of the Palestinian-Israeli conflict and of how to think theologically about it is thus inescapably and unapologetically shaped by these experiences and friendships. While this book is therefore not a neutral account, and while it starts from the assumption that Christian thinking about the Palestinian-Israeli conflict should privilege the voices and reflections of Palestinian Christians, it does strive to portray multiple perspectives on the conflict, including divergent theological assessments of the conflict, in an accurate and fair manner.

INHABITING THE LAND OF PALESTINE AND ISRAEL: TWO STORIES

Two stories illustrate the broader context of Palestinians and Israelis seeking secure dwellings in the land. The first story comes from a windswept hilltop in the northern Galilee, close to Israel's border with Lebanon. On this hill, a group of young adults in 2013 set up a makeshift residence. Walaa Sbait, Amir Ashkar, and around twenty others sought to make a home in the ruins of their ancestral village, Iqrit. These young activists planted trees and a garden and set up homes amidst the ruins, using the still-intact church as a communal center. Sbait, Ashkar, and their friends are Palestinian Christians in their twenties and thirties who hold Israeli citizenship. Their parents and grandparents were expelled from Iqrit in 1948, along with the inhabitants of well over 400 Palestinian towns and villages depopulated during the 1948 Arab-Israeli war, a war called the War of Independence by Israelis and the *nakba*, or catastrophe, by Palestinians. Some expelled Iqritis ended up as refugees in Lebanon, while others stayed in the new State of Israel as internally displaced persons. The Israeli military later destroyed all of Iqrit's buildings, except for its Greek Catholic church.

Over the past seven decades, the uprooted villagers of Iqrit have waged a nonviolent struggle to be allowed to return to their lands and village. While Israel's High Court ruled that the Palestinians expelled from Iqrit and another Christian village in the northern Galilee, Kafr Bir'im, should be allowed back to their village lands, the Israeli military has persisted in preventing them from returning, even as the state turned over some of Iqrit's lands to Israeli agricultural communities (*moshavim*). Starting in the 1970s, Iqritis began holding summer camps amidst the village's ruins as a way of nurturing the connection of younger generations to their ancestral land. Some of Iqrit's families met with Pope Francis during his visit to the Holy Land in 2014 to share the village's story. The ongoing efforts of those displaced from Iqrit to return to their ancestral lands reflect the broader attempts by displaced Palestinians—both Christians and Muslims—to come home from exile. The insistent struggle by Iqrit's former inhabitants and their descendants also exemplifies the broader insistence of Palestinian Christians that they have a rightful place in the land and will struggle to maintain it.

The second story is that of Eitan Bronstein. Born into an Argentinian Jewish family in the early 1960s, Eitan and his parents made *aliyah* to Israel when Eitan was five years old. *Aliyah* is a Hebrew word that literally means "ascent" and more prosaically refers to immigration to Israel. The description of immigration to Israel as *aliyah* reflects a Zionist understanding of Jewish settlement in the land of Israel as an exalted task, the ending of Jewish exile and the fulfillment of Jewish identity and destiny. Eitan and his family moved into a communal settlement called a *kibbutz*. Eitan recalls climbing around what he assumed were centuries-old ruins during his childhood in Kibbutz Bahan.

As an adult, Eitan became involved in efforts to foster dialogue encounters between Israeli Jews and Palestinians. He also discovered that the ruins around his boyhood home of Kibbutz Bahan belonged to the Palestinian village of Qaqun, a village that, like Iqrit, was destroyed in 1948. Eitan began to reflect on the relationship between Palestinian refugees uprooted in 1948 from villages like Qaqun and durable peacebuilding between Israelis and Palestinians. While Israeli Jews typically view the Palestinian insistence on the right of refugees to return to the homes from which they were displaced as an existential threat, Eitan started wondering if provoking conversations within Israeli society about Palestinian refugee return might be an essential component to durable peacebuilding. These reflections led Eitan to join others in founding Zochrot, an organization dedicated to "remembering the *nakba* in Hebrew." Zochrot regularly organizes visits to the sites of destroyed Palestinian villages, including Iqrit, for groups of Israelis, where they learn about the villages' histories and post signs in Arabic and Hebrew marking the villages' ruins. When possible, displaced Palestinians from these villages join Zochrot in these actions.

These two stories are, of course, a miniscule selection from the millions of individual Palestinian and Israeli stories. Given the diverse histories of the people living in Palestine and Israel, no one or two stories will be completely representative. However, the stories of Eitan, Zochrot, and the displaced people of Iqrit are illustrative of the intertwined histories of Zionism and Palestinian dispossession. Taken together, these stories highlight the fact that the questions of what inhabiting the land means and what secure dwellings for Palestinians and Israelis might look like are central to understanding the Palestinian-Israeli conflict.

These two stories also suggest that a caveat about the framing device I have used throughout the book of a "conflict" between the "intertwined" histories of Zionism and Palestinian nationalism is in order. From one angle, to describe the confrontation between the Zionist movement and the Palestinian national movement as a "conflict" and to portray Palestinian and Zionist histories as "intertwined" might appear to portray a confrontation between two equal parties with two equally legitimate claims. Such a framing is not my intent. The Palestinian-Israeli conflict should not be viewed as a contest between two equal parties, but rather as a confrontation between a late form of European settler-colonialism (Zionism) and an anti-colonial movement against Ottoman, British, and Zionist forces (Palestinian nationalism), a confrontation that has resulted in ongoing Palestinian dispossession. Palestinian and Israeli Jewish identities should not be understood as solely reactive to one another, yet their stories have also undoubtedly been intertwined and have shaped one other. The stories of Iqrit and Zochrot open up the fragile hope and tentative possibility that alternative ways of inhabiting the land, alternative forms of dwelling in the land that disrupt and transcend colonial histories and structures that perpetuate dispossession, are possible.

CHAPTER OUTLINE

The ensuing chapters dig deeper into the historical roots and the contemporary manifestations of the conflict between Palestinians and Israelis over inhabiting the land. Chapter 1 examines Zionism and Palestinian nationalism as two intertwined phenomena. Beginning with their inception in the late nineteenth and early twentieth centuries, this chapter explores the competing Zionist and Palestinian nationalist narratives of the twentieth century into the present, discussing how a story of national liberation from the Zionist perspective has been experienced as a *nakba*, or catastrophe, by Palestinians. The chapter introduces readers to Zionism's emergence within the coalescing realities of European nationalism, colonialism, and rising anti-Semitism in the nineteenth century and to the diversity of Zionist visions. The chapter also presents different forms of Palestinian nationalism, including Islamist movements such as Hamas. Through this discussion of Zionism and Palestinian nationalism, the reader will also be introduced to the basic history of the Palestinian-Israeli conflict. A detailed timeline and a set of maps at the end of this book supplement this historical overview.

In chapter 2, the focus shifts from historical narration and analysis to theological interpretations of that history. Specifically, this chapter provides an overview of Palestinian Christian theologies that emerged in the latter half of the twentieth century as Palestinian Christians sought to understand Zionism and Palestinian dispossession theologically. The chapter examines how Palestinian Christian theology is marked by narratives of dispossession and by assertions of belonging in the land and breaks down key theological issues with which Palestinian Christian theologians grapple. The reader will encounter distinct streams of Palestinian Christian theology, including liberation and contextual theologies. The chapter also examines ecumenical Palestinian initiatives such as Kairos Palestine and its call to the worldwide church to stand with the Palestinian church and to support Palestinians and Israelis working for a future of justice and peace for all in the land.

In chapter 3 the lens expands and draws back to place Palestinian Christian theology within broader Christian assessments of Zionism and attempts to rethink Christian theologies of the Jewish people. The chapter begins with an overview of the roots and present shape of Christian Zionism and the privileged place it gives to the return of the Jewish people to the land within salvation history. I trace the origins of Christian Zionism and explore the global reach of Christian Zionist theology, after which I turn to Palestinian Christian objections to Christian Zionism. The chapter next examines how, following the Holocaust, Catholic and Protestant churches undertook a reassessment of traditional theologies of repudiation or replacement of the Jewish people. This revisioning involved articulating how God remains in covenant relationship with the Jewish people. For some theologians, this theological revisioning process went hand-in-hand with theological affirmations and defenses of the new State of Israel, while others struggled to hold together theological reassessments of Judaism with criticism of Israeli state policies and with a commitment to justice for Palestinians. The chapter concludes with an exploration of how one particular Palestinian Christian theologian, Michel Sabbah, the first Palestinian to serve as Latin (Roman Catholic) Patriarch of Jerusalem, has responded to Christian Zionism and how he has advanced a critique of Zionism and Israeli state practices within the context of broader Catholic teachings about Judaism and Jewish-Christian relations. Through this chapter, the reader will gain a deeper appreciation for the complex ways that Christian theological assessments of Judaism and Zionism have been intertwined and for attempts to disentangle them.

The fourth and final chapter turns to the present, outlining the key issues at stake in the current form of the Palestinian-Israeli conflict and assessing the moribund Israeli-Palestinian peace process and its prospects for revival. The chapter introduces readers to why some Palestinians and Israelis increasingly claim that two-state approaches to the Palestinian-Israeli conflict have been eclipsed and to rejoinders that such two-state visions remain the only viable hope for a resolution to the conflict. The chapter concludes with some constructive thoughts about what inhabiting the land rightly will entail for Israelis and Palestinians, thoughts that build upon insights from Palestinian Christian theologies of *sumud*, or steadfastness.

KEY TERMINOLOGY USED IN THIS BOOK

Throughout the book, I introduce terms specific to the Palestinian-Israeli conflict, defining most of them upon first use. Some terms, however, are so foundational to the book as a whole that it is beneficial to provide cursory explanations of the terms upfront. Such basic definitions—which I will flesh out in greater detail over the coming chapters—are offered in this section.

Zionism

One way to understand Zionism is as a late form of European nationalism. Just as German and French nationalism in the early nineteenth century imagined German and French nations whose territorial self-expressions were bound up with the German and French states, so Zionism imagined Jewish identity as needing to be expressed territorially and secured by a Jewish state. Another way to understand Zionism is as an internally diverse movement to revive Jewish life within *eretz yisrael*, the biblical land of Israel.

Zionism, as will be seen in chapter 1, was a diverse movement from its inception. Some Zionists were religious, while others were secular. Some were socialists, but by no means all. While the majority were focused on the establishment of a Jewish state, some viewed Zionism as a movement for cultural renewal in the land. Chapter 3 will examine Christian Zionism as a Christian theological affirmation of Jewish return to the land.

Israel, Palestine, Occupied Territories

How to name the land inhabited by Israelis and Palestinians—indeed, how to name those inhabitants themselves—is a point of contention. Throughout this book I refer to "Palestine and Israel" to name the territory that lies between the Jordan River to the east and the Mediterranean Sea to the west, extending from the Gulf of Aqaba in the south to a border with Lebanon in the north. I use the name Palestine and Israel in recognition of the national aspirations of Palestinians and Israelis, aspirations bound up with the vision of secure statehood encapsulated by the names Palestine and Israel. Sometimes I will use "the land" as a shorthand for the entirety of Palestine and Israel.

In addition to being used as a geographical marker in Roman antiquity onwards, the term Palestine carries multiple modern meanings. It stands as the name for the nation to which Palestinian Arabs understand themselves to belong. It refers to the state that Palestinian nationalists sought to establish in part of the former Ottoman Empire beginning in the early twentieth century. Mandate Palestine names the territory between the Jordan River to the east and the Mediterranean Sea to the west that Great Britain controlled after being given a "mandate" by the League of Nations to administer that portion of the defeated Ottoman Empire. While there is no sovereign state of Palestine (in the sense of a state that exercises full self-governance over its territory and its borders), the United Nations General Assembly in 2012 extended *de facto*, albeit not *de jure* (with the binding force of law), recognition to the State of Palestine. Over 130 countries around the world have recognized the State of Palestine. When Palestinians refer to Palestine today, they can mean multiple things. They might be referring to the entire land of Mandate Palestine or to the sovereign state that Palestinians seek to establish within the West Bank, East Jerusalem, and the Gaza Strip, or to the Palestinian National Authority (PA), set up as part of the Oslo peace process, which exercises limited autonomy in the Occupied Territories.

Israel in this book will typically refer to the modern State of Israel, a state that defines itself as the state of the Jewish people. Since 1967, this state has controlled all the territory of Mandate Palestine. Uses of "Israel" to refer to the biblical people called Israel or to the biblical "land of Israel," or *eretz yisrael*, will be clearly marked. For some Israelis, Israel refers only to the 78 percent of Mandate Palestine comprising the State of Israel recognized by the United Nations. For others, it refers to all of Mandate Palestine.

The phrase Occupied Territories here refers to the 22 percent of Mandate Palestine consisting of East Jerusalem, the West Bank, and the Gaza Strip conquered by Israel in 1967. (During that war, Israel also occupied the Sinai Peninsula from Egypt, which it returned in 1982 as part of the Egyptian-Israeli peace treaty signed in 1979, and the Golan

Heights from Syria, which it still controls and has annexed.) After the conquests, some Israelis began establishing settlements in these territories, a process that has accelerated over the past decades.

Israel refers to these territories as "administered," arguing that they are not "occupied" because there was no legitimate sovereign power for these lands prior to them being captured by Israel. The United Nations, however, along with the vast majority of international law scholars and practically all countries of the world, including the United States, do view East Jerusalem, the West Bank, and the Gaza Strip as militarily occupied territory.

The people who identify as Palestinian are dispersed geographically. Over four million Palestinians live in the West Bank, East Jerusalem, and the Gaza Strip. Millions of Palestinians from what has become Israel live as refugees in United Nations-administered camps in Jordan, Syria, Lebanon, and the Occupied Territories. Israeli laws, walls, and the infrastructure of Israel's military occupation, with its checkpoints, roadblocks, and more, separate Palestinians from one another.

Because the State of Israel defines itself as the state of the Jewish people, even as some non-Jews hold Israeli citizenship, the meaning of the term Israeli is sometimes ambiguous. On the one hand, Israeli is often used in popular discourse to refer to Jews with Israeli citizenship. More broadly, however, Israeli refers to anyone holding Israeli citizenship. This group includes people whom the Israeli state refers to as Israeli Arab. The people designated as Israeli Arab, however, increasingly identify themselves as Palestinian citizens of Israel.

Anti-Semitism and Anti-Judaism

In this book, anti-Semitism refers to hostility toward or prejudice against Jews as a religious or ethnic group. Some commentators observe that the term Semites designates people who speak a Semitic language such as Hebrew or Arabic, and that anti-Semitism thus includes hostility towards Arabs. That said, this book follows the predominant usage of the term anti-Semitism as referring to prejudice and hatred towards Jews. Anti-Judaism, meanwhile, here refers to negative Christian theological judgments about the status of the Jewish people before God. Throughout Western Christian history, anti-Judaism and anti-Semitism have been distinct, yet often intertwined, realities.

HOW NOT TO TALK ABOUT THE PALESTINIAN-ISRAELI CONFLICT

To write or talk about the Palestinian-Israeli conflict can feel like entering a rhetorical minefield, where one wrong word or phrase will trigger explosive objections. The temptations, in turn, are to become paralyzed or to avoid the topic altogether, out of fear of giving offense. While anything written about the Israeli-Palestinian conflict will inevitably generate strong critiques from one quarter or another, some ways of thinking and talking about the conflict are clearly problematic because they trade in harmful stereotypes and because they prevent a nuanced assessment of a complex reality. The following guidelines name some of these problematic approaches in order to promote more careful and constructive reflection about the Palestinian-Israeli conflict and its possible transformation.

Don't deny Palestinian or Jewish attachment to the land.

Sadly, much writing about the Palestinian-Israeli conflict proceeds by denying the attachment of one of the parties to the land. One strain of pro-Israeli argument, thoroughly discredited in academic circles, simply denies the existence of distinct Palestinian national identity or claims that Palestinian Arabs do not have centuries-long connections to the land. One recent version of this spurious argument gained publicity when someone began selling a blank book purporting to tell the history of the Palestinian people, with the blankness of the pages a testament to the supposed lack of Palestinian identity and history.

Some pro-Palestinian writing, meanwhile, presents Jewish attachment to the land as inauthentic or illegitimate. A valid recognition of Zionism's structural similarities to settler-colonial movements bleeds into a problematic rejection of Jewish bonds to the land, a move that ignores the long-standing presence of Jewish communities in the land as well as the enduring place of the land in the prayers of diaspora Jewish communities across the centuries.

Approaches to the Palestinian-Israeli conflict that deny the existence of one of the parties or that reject as inauthentic the bonds one of the parties feels to the land are not constructive and do not make for peace. In extreme forms, such denial is wedded to political visions of expelling (or, put euphemistically, "transferring") the other party from the land. To be sure, the recognition by both parties of each other's existence and the reality of the other's attachment to the land does not, by itself, dictate answers the Palestinian-Israeli conflict. Should common attachments to the land be expressed through two separate nation-states (as in so-called "two-state solutions")? Through shared citizenship in one state? Or through some other configuration?

People of good will can and do differ on such questions. But mutual recognition of one another's bond to the land is an essential prerequisite to any durable resolution to the conflict.

Avoid anti-Semitic, anti-Arab, and anti-Muslim stereotypes.

It should go without saying that one should refrain from using harmful stereotypes, yet in speaking in church, academic, and other settings about the Palestinian-Israeli conflict over the years, I have been distressed by how often audience members resort to such stereotypes. Palestinians are tarred with anti-Muslim and anti-Arab stereotypes of being inherently violent and irrational. Critiques of Israel are couched in terms of vicious anti-Semitic stereotypes of Jews as greedy or of Jews as exercising secretive, global control over politics, culture, and the economy. As with all stereotypes, these prejudicial portrayals of Israeli Jews and Palestinians both preclude a clear, sober assessment of reality and actively perpetuate harm.

Don't assume that Palestinians and Israeli Jews are homogeneous.

Like all groups of people, Israeli Jews and Palestinians represent a wide diversity of perspectives and histories. Be it diversity of religious convictions and practice, political commitments, localized identities, family backgrounds, and much more—Palestinian and Israeli Jewish identities are richly diverse. While it is inevitable in an introductory book like this to refer to large group identities such as Israeli Jewish and Palestinian, readers should remember that behind such large group identities stand complex realities.

Don't conflate Judaism and Zionism; do recognize diversity within Judaism and Zionism.

Not all Jews are Zionists. Some Jewish groups, like the Satmar Hasidim, oppose Zionism as blasphemous, arguing that the re-establishment of a divinely-approved Jewish state will only occur with the arrival of the *mashiach*, or messiah. Other Jewish groups critique Zionism as conflicting with prophetic calls for justice in the *Tanakh*, or Hebrew Bible (what Christians have traditionally called the Old Testament). Some Jews are non-Zionist, in that Zionism is simply not part of their Jewish identity. Others are anti-Zionist, actively opposing Zionism on Jewish grounds.

Just as the diversity of perspectives among Jews regarding Zionism should be recognized, so should the diversity of thought among self-identified Zionists be acknowledged. The first chapter includes an examination of different types of Zionism, along with an overview of Jewish critics of Zionism.

Don't assume that critiques of the State of Israel or Zionism are anti-Semitic.

Advocates for the State of Israel and of Zionism often portray criticisms of Israeli state actions and Zionism as motivated by an anti-Semitic hostility towards Jews. Why are Israeli human rights abuses highlighted while others are ignored?, Israel's defenders will sometimes ask. Regarding Zionism, its proponents will sometimes ask its opponents why Jewish self-determination, unlike French or German self-determination, comes under criticism, suggesting that anti-Semitism must be the answer. Such defenders of the State of Israel and Zionism in turn portray Jewish critics of Israeli practices and Zionism as self-hating Jews.

Anti-Semitic attitudes and rhetoric do undeniably surface within some critiques of Israeli state practices and Zionism: when anti-Semitism arises, it must be vigorously opposed. At the same time, however, accusations by pro-Israel advocates of anti-Semitism often operate to discredit or cast suspicion upon all critique of Israeli state practices and Zionism. The Palestinian Christian theologies to be examined in the ensuing chapters exemplify the fact that one can be critical of Israeli state policies and actions and Zionism while also rigorously guarding against anti-Semitism.

Don't decontextualize acts of violence.

The first thoughts many people have of the Palestinian-Israeli conflict are of specific acts of deadly violence: the wars of 1948 and 1967; suicide bombings carried out by Hamas on a public bus or in a crowded market in Israel; Israel's bombardment of the Gaza Strip; crude rockets fired by Islamists from Gaza into Israel; an Israeli settler arson attack on a West Bank home that leaves a Palestinian infant dead; the list could go on. For Christians, each death resulting from these acts of violence is to be mourned as the loss of a person created in God's image.

However, gaining a deeper understanding of the Palestinian-Israeli conflict requires viewing specific acts of deadly violence within the broader context of the clash between two intertwined nationalist movements, a clash between a Zionist movement seeking security and freedom for the Jewish people within an independent nation-state and a Palestinian national movement that has experienced this Zionist movement as a settler-colonial project bound up with Palestinian dispossession. To be sure, both Zionist and Palestinian nationalist movements advance justifications for the acts of deadly violence committed by their partisans and both appeal to memories of deadly violence they have faced in order to mobilize their supporters and to justify new acts of violence. Yet a focus on specific acts of violence can lead to distorted analysis of the conflict: first, because such a focus decontextualizes specific acts of violence from their broader histories; and second, because a focus on deadly, extraordinary violence can lead one to overlook the ways in which state power operates daily within Israel and the Occupied Territories to dispossess Palestinians and to constrain movement and economic possibilities through arbitrary detention, land confiscation, zoning restrictions, declaring certain areas to be closed military zones, construction and maintenance of a network of checkpoints and roadblocks, and more.

As will be discussed further in chapter 2, Palestinian Christian theologians have overwhelmingly advocated for nonviolent resistance to Israel's military occupation and have lamented and mourned deaths from the conflict—even as they have highlighted the routinized violence that Palestinians face every day and have protested what they perceive as a global double standard that pays greater attention to the loss of Israeli than Palestinian life.

Don't describe the Palestinian-Israeli conflict as an ancient, age-old conflict.

Lazy pundits and comedians routinely make tired jokes about or references to an intractable Israeli-Palestinian conflict stretching back for centuries or even millennia. Such characterizations of the conflict are problematic on several levels. First, and most importantly, depictions of the conflict as ancient are simply wrong on historical grounds. Rather than being ancient, the Israeli-Palestinian conflict is a thoroughly modern phenomenon, stemming from the late nineteenth and early twentieth century. Zionism, while indeed drawing upon and transforming Jewish eschatological hopes of a redemptive return to Zion, bears family resemblances to modern European nationalism and settler-colonialism, while Palestinian nationalism emerges contemporaneously with modern Arab nationalism.

Not only are descriptions of the conflict as ancient—and therefore intractable—historically mistaken, they draw upon racist stereotypes and harmful assumptions. The portrayal of ancient hatreds animating the conflict trade upon racist depictions of Arabs and the "Middle East" as particularly prone to violent, irrational conflict (in contrast to a supposedly less violent, more rational, and secular or Christian West).

Furthermore, talk of age-old enmity presents the Israeli-Palestinian conflict as uniquely intractable, with efforts to resolve or transform it deemed hopeless from the start. One can recognize the conflict's complexity and the despair such complexity can breed while still holding out hope for the transformation of the Israeli-Palestinian conflict, a hope informed by examples of other supposedly intractable conflicts in the modern era undergoing substantive transformation (such as the fall of the apartheid regime in South Africa). To be sure, good grounds exist for being soberly skeptical of grandiose visions of social transformation. Post-apartheid South Africa, for example, continues in many ways to be shaped by racist, colonial legacies, while the United States in the post–Jim Crow, post–Civil Rights movement era remains a country in which white supremacy shapes American institutions and communities. Yet the complexity of conflicts and the ability of oppressive systems to morph into new forms should not blind one to signs of hope. Put theologically, the enduring strength of the powers and principalities that cling so closely to our social and individual bodies should not lead us to despair, but should keep us prayerfully alert for and expectant of the in-breaking of God's redeeming Spirit.

QUESTIONS FOR DISCUSSION

1. Have you visited Palestine and Israel before? Have you met Israelis or Palestinians? Have pastors in your church ever preached about the State of Israel and the Israeli-Palestinian conflict? What prior associations do you have regarding the Palestinian-Israeli conflict?

2. Is thinking theologically about the Palestinian-Israeli conflict different from how Christians should think about conflicts over land generally? If not, why? If so, how?

3. Define anti-Semitism.

4. What does the term Occupied Territories designate? What does the State of Israel call the Occupied Territories?

1

ZIONISM AND PALESTINIAN NATIONALISM: INTERTWINED HISTORIES

THIS CHAPTER TRACES THE roots of the Palestinian-Israeli conflict by examining the histories of Zionism and Palestinian nationalism. In the course of narrating these intertwined histories, the chapter provides a mostly chronological account of the Palestinian-Israeli conflict from the late nineteenth century up to the present. This historical narrative is supplemented by the timeline in Appendix 1. Readers interested in exploring the history of the Palestinian-Israeli conflict in greater depth should consult the studies listed in the Further Reading section at the end of this book.

ZIONISM AND EUROPEAN NATIONALISM

Zionism is a modern nationalist movement originating in the late nineteenth century. Most versions of Zionism aimed at securing Jewish sovereignty and reviving Jewish life within Palestine in what was then part of the Ottoman Empire. Zionism thus emerged late within the rise of European nationalism in the 1800s, during which time questions of national identity and roots became increasingly pronounced. As states became focused on answering these questions of identity (What does it mean to be French? to be German? etc.), the place of Jews within European society became a point of debate and contention. Traditionally confined primarily to ghettos, some European Jews started becoming assimilated into broader national contexts. Yet even as this assimilation process unfolded, some European Jews had become convinced that Jewish assimilation into their broader societies within contexts of rising nationalist sentiment was an illusory dream. In 1862, Jewish philosopher Moshe Hess published *Rome and Jerusalem*, in which he envisioned the establishment of a Jewish socialist commonwealth in the land. Anti-Jewish pogroms, or riots, in 1881 in Tsarist Russia set off an initial wave of Zionist migration (*aliyah*, or ascent) to Palestine. In 1882, Judah Pinsker penned one of the first Zionist tracts, *Auto-Emancipation*, in which he argued that the Jewish people were a distinctive element among the European nations who could not be assimilated. Therefore, he continued, Jews needed to take responsibility for their own future and find a place where they could exercise self-determination free from other nations.

Alongside other languages, most Eastern European Jews at this time spoke Yiddish, a Germanic dialect with borrowings from biblical Hebrew and from various

European languages. The linguist Eliezer Ben-Yehuda, who immigrated to Palestine in 1881, argued that the Zionist vision required the revival of Hebrew as a spoken, instead of solely liturgical, language. Ben-Yehuda and fellow collaborators simplified Hebrew grammar, invented new Hebrew words, and created the first Hebrew dictionary. The Modern Hebrew spoken in Israel today has its origins in the efforts of this group.

By the late nineteenth century, Zionist energies had begun to coalesce. The Dreyfus Affair, in which Albert Dreyfus, a French military officer of Jewish descent, was accused in 1894 of spying for Germany, exposed a strong current of anti-Semitism running through French society (and through Europe more broadly). By 1896, Theodor Herzl, one of the leading intellectual visionaries of Zionism, had shifted from staunch advocacy of assimilation into European societies to a firmly pro-Zionist position, a shift represented in Herzl's influential tome, *Der Judenstaat* (The Jewish State). In 1897, Herzl convened the First Zionist Congress in Basel, Switzerland, joined by other early Zionist luminaries like Max Nordau. The meeting produced the pioneering Basel Program, which articulated the vision of establishing a national home of the Jewish people in *eretz yisrael* (the biblical "land of Israel") and a program of encouraging the settlement of Jewish farmers, manufacturers, and artisans in the land. While Herzl and other early Zionists sometimes entertained ideas of the Zionist project unfolding in other locations, such as Uganda, the primary focus of Zionist territorial aspirations was the land of Israel. A phrase from Herzl's writings—"If you will it, it is no dream"—captured Zionism's Romantic and visionary spirit, becoming a widely used Zionist slogan.

The next two decades witnessed accelerated developments in the Zionist project. The period between 1904 and 1914 witnessed a second wave of *aliyah*, with around 35,000 Jews, mostly from Eastern Europe, immigrating to Palestine. Two key events then transpired during World War I that proved momentous. In 1916, as it became clear that the Ottoman Empire, led from Istanbul, was on the brink of defeat, British and French officials, led by Mark Sykes and François Georges-Picot, met in secret to agree on the division of the Arab Middle East into respective French and British spheres of control. Then, in 1917, the United Kingdom's Foreign Secretary Arthur Balfour wrote a letter to a leading Zionist in Britain, Walter Rothschild, in which he committed the United Kingdom to a policy of support for Zionist aspirations. The pertinent section of the letter, which came popularly to be known as the Balfour Declaration, expressed the United Kingdom's support for "the establishment in Palestine of a national home for the Jewish people," so long as it does not "prejudice the civil and religious rights of existing non-Jewish communities in Palestine, or the rights and political status enjoyed by Jews in any other country."[1]

In the wake of World War I, a third wave of approximately 40,000 Jewish immigrants moved to Palestine. The vast majority of these immigrants came from Eastern Europe following the October Revolution of 1917–1918 in Russia. Then, in 1922, the newly formed League of Nations granted Britain a Mandate over the parts of the dissolved Ottoman Empire called Palestine and Transjordan (today's Jordan). The League of Nations also granted Britain a Mandate over Iraq and France a Mandate over Lebanon and Syria. As Mandate powers, Britain and France were tasked with administering these former Ottoman territories for a transitional period towards national independence and

1. Full text of the Balfour Declaration available at the Avalon Project, avalon.law.yale.edu/20th_century/balfour.asp.

self-determination. The Mandate system reflected colonial assumptions that Western powers had a "civilizing mission" to prepare non-Western peoples for self-determination. British authorities ruled Palestine for more than a quarter century, with the Mandate ending in 1948.

DIVERSITIES OF ZIONISM

From its inception, Zionism was an internally diverse movement, with different visions for Jewish settlement in *eretz yisrael*. Key streams within Zionism included:

Labor Zionism

One major current of Zionist thought sought to merge socialist ideals with the Zionist project of establishing a Jewish state. Key leaders included Nachman Syrkin, Haim Orlosoroff, and Berl Katznelson. The State of Israel's first Prime Minister, David Ben-Gurion, emerged from this so-cialist stream of Zionism—as did Israel's Labor Party.

Labor Zionists held that worldwide socialist revolu-tions would not solve the question of the place of Jews with-in their broader nation-states—an independent Jewish state was still needed. "Hebrew Labor" (*avodah ivrit*) would be essential to the establishment of such a state, Labor Zionists insisted. The iconic Israeli institution of the *kibbutzim*—collective communities—emerged from this movement.

Revisionist Zionism

Led by Ze'ev Jabotinsky, Revisionist Zionists chafed at what they viewed as compromising tactics of Zionist leaders like Chaim Weizmann and David Ben-Gurion, who argued that the Zionist movement should take a practical approach and accept sovereignty in whatever parts of *eretz yisrael* would be granted by the ruling authorities. Revisionists like Jabotinsky, in contrast, advanced a maximalist approach, pressing British authorities for Jewish settlement not only in Palestine, but also in Transjordan (east of the Jordan River), where the British Mandate rulers had prevented Zionist settlement.

Revisionist Zionists were staunch anti-communists and regularly came into conflict with Labor Zionists. Future Israeli Prime Ministers Menachem Begin and Yitzhak Shamir emerged from within the Revisionist movement, leading paramilitary organizations (Irgun and Lehi, respectively) that attacked British authorities and Palestinian Arabs. Today's Likud party is a descendant of Revisionist Zionism.

Religious Zionism

Jewish life in Palestine during the Ottoman era was concentrated in what came to be known as the four holy cities of Jerusalem, Hebron, Safed, and Tiberias. Yet while these Jewish communities lived and prayed in *eretz yisrael*, they viewed themselves, like other religious Jews, as being in a state of exile, awaiting the coming of the *mashiach*, or messiah, and the ingathering of the exiles and the establishment of the messianic kingdom. Attempts to establish a Jewish state prior to the messiah's coming, from this perspective, were blasphemous.

The religious Zionism propounded by Rabbi Abraham Isaac Kook (1865–1935) broke from this traditional understanding of Jewish return to the land. For Kook, Zionism, even as a secular movement, was part of a divine plan to bring God's chosen people back to the land, where they would be able to follow laws of the Torah and observe halakhic precepts (rabbinic law as identified in the Talmud) specific to life in *eretz yisrael*. Kook and his followers maintained that Zionist settlement, rather than expressing a blasphemous repudiation of divine will, represented a faithful anticipation of and preparation for the messiah's return. Abraham Isaac Kook's son, Rabbi Zvi Yehuda Kook, further developed his father's religious nationalist ideas, but with a greater emphasis on militarism and political action. In the 1970s, groups like Gush Emunim (Bloc of the Faithful) that pressed for Israeli settlement and even annexation of the Occupied Territories took inspiration from Zvi Yehuda Kook's ideas. The younger Kook's ideas in turn paved the way for figures such as Rabbi Meir Kahane, an outspoken advocate for the expulsion of Palestinians from *eretz yisrael*. The legacy of Kook lives on today among religious West Bank settlers and the right-wing HaBayit HaYehudi (Our Jewish Home) party.

Cultural Zionism

For the cultural Zionism espoused by Ahad Ha'am, a leader in the World Zionist Organization in the early twentieth century, the Zionist project's focus was to be on the revival of Jewish culture and the Hebrew language as a living language (rather than solely a language of worship and prayer) within *eretz yisrael*. Contrary to Herzl's flexibility about the location of the envisioned Jewish state, Ha'am insisted on Palestine as the only option for the Zionist project, while also stressing the importance of Jewish self-reliance in reviving Jewish life in the land.

Cultural Zionists like Ha'am were not necessarily opposed to the eventual establishment of a Jewish state—but they wanted to ensure that such a state would truly be a Jewish state in terms of culture and values, rather than simply a state of the Jews, and so emphasized the primary importance of Jewish spiritual revival in the land.

Brit Shalom and Proponents of Binationalism

Ha'am's ideas were taken up by a small group of intellectuals in Mandate Palestine who banded together in 1925 to found Brit Shalom (Covenant of Peace). While small, Brit Shalom's membership included prominent Jewish academics like Arthur Ruppin and Martin Buber. Like Ha'am, the Brit Shalom circle envisioned Zionism as focused on the renewal of Jewish cultural life in the land. To that emphasis, Brit Shalom added the espousal of a binational state in which Jews and Palestinian Arabs would hold equal citizenship. While the Brit Shalom circle was short-lived, dissolving in the early 1930s, some of its members, joined by Judah Magnes, then-president of Hebrew University, established the Ihud political party, which also advocated for a binational state for Palestinians and Jews.

ZIONISM AS POLITICAL THEOLOGY AND ITS CRITICS

Israeli political theorist Amnon Raz-Krakotzkin has argued that a particular political theology is embedded within most Zionist visions. Zionism, he contends, upends and transforms traditional Jewish understandings of exile, return, and redemption into a political theology founded on three main pillars: the negation of exile (*shelilat ha-galut*); the return to the land (*ha-shiva la-eretz yisrael*); and the return to history (*ha-shiva la-historia*). Within this Zionist political theology, Raz-Krakotzkin maintains, Jewish exile is transformed from a condition of expectant longing for redemption and the Messiah's coming into a diseased state of weakness to be overcome by a return to the land of Israel and a return to a history of sovereign rule. Raz-Krakotzkin thus claims that while many Zionists may have understood themselves as non-religious or as atheists, their Zionism was shaped by a radical transformation of traditional Jewish concepts, thus representing a secularized political theology.[2]

As a significant transformation of traditional Jewish concepts and commitments, Zionism was slow to find a foothold within Jewish communities globally and encountered significant resistance. As noted above, Orthodox and ultra-Orthodox Jewish groups opposed Zionism on the grounds that it represented a blasphemous lack of faith in God's sovereignty. Some ultra-Orthodox Jewish groups, such as the Satmar Hasidim, continue this staunch anti-Zionist opposition. Other Jewish critics of Zionism have drawn upon the Jewish tradition of prophetic denunciation of injustice, universalist streams within Judaism, or socialist or revolutionary ideals. So, for example, from the 1960s to the 1980s the Israeli revolutionary socialist organization, Matzpen, articulated a consistent anti-Zionist stance and advanced a vigorous critique of the occupation. Today, an organization such as Jewish Voice for Peace in the United States stakes out anti-Zionist positions in its activism against the occupation and for Palestinian human rights.

THE EMERGENCE OF PALESTINIAN NATIONALISM AND ZIONIST RESISTANCE TO BRITISH RULE

Just as European nationalism arose during the nineteenth century, so did a distinct Arab national identity begin to

2. Raz-Krakotzkin, *Exil et Souveraineté*, 27

coalesce within the Ottoman Empire during this time period, alongside more regionally focused identities, including Palestinian national identity. Palestinians proudly highlight centuries-old family histories in the land; Zionists, meanwhile, underscore the enduring place of Jerusalem and the land within Jewish liturgy and prayers over the centuries. While these enduring historical connections of Jews and Palestinians to the land are very real, Zionism and Palestinian nationalism, like all nationalisms, are modern movements. Rashid Khalidi argues that Palestinian national identity as it emerged in the late nineteenth and early twentieth centuries should be analyzed in terms of sets of overlapping identities: people understood their identities in localized terms (e.g., coming from the Nablus area), in a national (Palestinian) context, in a broader regional perspective (Greater Syria, or *balad ash-sham*), and in religious terms (Muslim, Christian, etc.). Like Zionism and other forms of nationalism, Palestinian nationalism should be understood as the modern formation of what Benedict Anderson has called "imagined communities." While nationalists often portray their nations as ancient and primordial (something done by both Zionists and Palestinian nationalists), they are in fact modern developments, new forms of association and solidarity.

Khalidi rightly contends that Palestinian nationalism should not be reductively explained as a reaction to Zionism. At the same time, Khalidi also correctly acknowledges that Zionist settlement in Palestine in the late 1800s and early 1900s helped to spur the development of Palestinian national identity. Palestinians quickly became concerned about Zionist settlement. These concerns escalated with the collapse of the Ottoman Empire, the institution of British rule, and news spreading of the British promise in the Balfour Declaration of support for the establishment of a

Jewish national home in Palestine. The Balfour Declaration's commitment, Palestinian leaders worried, threatened their hopes for self-determination. The advent of British rule witnessed the founding of Muslim-Christian Associations in major Palestinian cities, leading to the convening of a Palestine Arab Congress in 1919 that called for representative government in Palestine and proclaimed opposition to the Balfour Declaration. Palestinian Christians have been leading thinkers and political figures within the Palestinian national movement from its earliest years (just as Arab Christians have played significant roles within Arab national movements more broadly).

As Zionist settlement expanded in the 1920s and 1930s, Palestinian resistance and nationalist sentiment increased. Tensions between the Zionist and Palestinian national movements also flared, as did attacks on the British ruling authority. In 1929, conflicts over changes to the status quo governing Jewish practice at the Western Wall exploded into deadly riots, leaving scores of Jews and Palestinians dead and hundreds more wounded. The riots included the massacre of 67 members of the centuries-old Jewish community in Hebron (even as some Palestinian Muslims in Hebron sheltered and protected Jewish families from the violence). Israeli historian Hillel Cohen has referred to 1929 as "year zero" of the Palestinian-Israeli conflict, arguing that the violence of that year solidified communal identities on both sides and set the pattern for intercommunal tension and violence from then on.

Paramilitary activity by Zionist and Palestinian militias against each other and the British Mandatory power increased in 1930s. Palestinian nonviolent and armed resistance against the British culminated in the Great Arab Revolt of 1936 to 1939, a revolt brutally suppressed by the British authorities. Zionist leaders, meanwhile, chafed at what they viewed as unwarranted British restrictions on Jewish immigration to Palestine. These frustrations mounted as Nazi anti-Semitic measures intensified in the 1930s. Militias such as Irgun and Lehi organized to challenge what they viewed as the illegitimate British occupation of the land.

The British government, meanwhile, sought ways to manage or resolve the burgeoning conflict, efforts that in the end pleased no one. The 1937 Peel Commission proposed dividing Mandate Palestine into a Jewish state, a mandatory zone, and an Arab state linked to Transjordan (now Jordan): this proposal envisioned the transfer of over 200,000 Palestinians from the projected Jewish state, along with around one thousand Jews from the anticipated Arab state. A 1939 White Paper formulated by Neville Chamberlin's government proposed a Jewish national home (but not state) within Palestine and an independent Palestine within ten years. Neither Palestinian nor Zionist leaders found the White Paper proposal acceptable. As the horrors of the Holocaust became evident and as the United States closed its doors to Jewish immigration from Europe, Zionist pressures on the British authorities to allow greater Jewish immigration to Palestine mounted.

By the end of World War II, Britain turned to the newly created United Nations for assistance in extricating itself from its mandate over Palestine. In November of 1947, the United Nations General Assembly passed Resolution 181, commonly known as the Partition Plan, which called for the division of Mandate Palestine into independent Jewish and Arab states, with international control over the greater Jerusalem area (including Bethlehem) as a *corpus separatum* (a separate territory to be under international supervision).[3] The Partition Plan envisioned that

3. See Appendix 2, Map 1.

Palestinians living in the territory of the proposed Jewish state would be able to remain there, just as Jews living in the territory of the proposed Arab state would be able to stay. Palestinian political leadership rejected the partition plan, arguing against territorial division, as did Revisionist Zionists, who viewed the plan as an illegitimate abdication of Jewish territory, in particular the biblical Jewish heartland of Judea and Samaria (today's West Bank). Mainstream Zionist leaders led by David Ben-Gurion accepted the partition plan on tactical, pragmatic grounds.

The British Mandate for Palestine ended on May 14, 1948. That same day, Ben-Gurion, as leader of the Jewish Agency for Palestine and the World Zionist Organization, issued a declaration of Israel as an independent Jewish state. The ongoing fighting between Zionist and Palestinian militias that had been raging in the lead-up to the declaration then transformed into a regional war, with Egyptian, Jordanian, Syrian, and Iraqi forces joining the fray. By the war's end, Israel was left in control of 78 percent of Mandate Palestine (larger than the 56 percent allocated for the Jewish state by the partition plan), while Jordan held the West Bank and East Jerusalem and Egypt controlled the Gaza Strip.[4]

INDEPENDENCE OR *NAKBA*?

In the dominant Israeli narrative, the war of 1948 represented the culmination of a struggle for Jewish freedom and independence in the land, a struggle conducted against formidable odds. While Israelis thus refer to the war as the War of Independence, Palestinians, in contrast, refer to it with the Arabic word *nakba,* or catastrophe. The war was catastrophic, from the Palestinian perspective, in that

4. See Appendix 2, Map 2.

33

two-thirds of the Palestinian population (ca. 750,000 people) became refugees over the course of the fighting, with well over 400 Palestinian towns and villages depopulated. Most of these uprooted persons ended up as refugees outside the new State of Israel. Others remained in Israel as internally displaced people. Palestinians who remained in what had become the State of Israel lived under military rule until the mid-1960s, with nightly curfews and limited movement outside of their towns and villages. Palestinians argue that the *nakba* of 1948 has continued over the following seven decades up to the present, with Israeli laws, policies, and actions furthering Palestinian dispossession.

Prior to Israel's founding, most Jewish immigrants to the land were from Ashkenazi, or Central and Eastern European, background. The years following the war also witnessed the arrival of hundreds of thousands of Mizrahi Jews (Jews from North Africa and the Middle East) to the new State of Israel from countries like Yemen, Iraq, Egypt, and Morocco. Zionist and then Israeli bodies worked to encourage and facilitate such immigration through a variety of means. Meanwhile, some Arab countries pressured Jews to leave their native lands—in some cases even expelling them.

The dichotomy in how Palestinians and Israelis view the war of 1948 reflects a deeper divergence in how they view the Zionist project of establishing an independent Jewish state in Palestine. Within the Zionist narrative, Zionism entailed the return of a far-flung, oft-persecuted people to its land and the achievement of landed security within that land, with security guaranteed because Jews would no longer live as a minority population. For Palestinians, however, Zionism appeared as a colonial movement set on uprooting and displacing the native Arab Palestinian population.

The colonial nature of Zionism, from the Palestinian vantage point, was captured by the claim made by some Zionists that Palestine was a land without a people, to be settled by a people without a land (i.e., the Jewish people). Zionist leaders were of course well aware that there were people present in Palestine—but they did not view these people as a nation with a right to self-determination, and so conceptually erased Palestinians from view.

Given the fact that Palestinians lived all throughout Palestine, both Labor and Revisionist Zionists recognized that the establishment of a Jewish state, understood as a state in which a significant percentage of the population was Jewish, would require the displacement and dispossession of the Palestinian Arab population. Some Zionists used the euphemism of "transfer" to discuss such envisioned dispossession, with some suggesting that financial incentives might prompt Palestinians to leave voluntarily. While historians debate the extent to which the uprooting of Palestinians during the 1948 war reflected prior military planning, what appears undeniable is that the fulfillment of any Zionist vision wedded to establishing a decisive Jewish majority within a bounded territory would require the uprooting of Palestinians from that territory, given the fact that the Palestinian population was spread throughout the land.

In 1949, the United Nations General Assembly passed Resolution 194, stipulating that Palestinian refugees "wishing to return to their homes and live at peace with their neighbours should be permitted to do so at the earliest practicable date."[5] In 1950, the UN established the United Nations Relief and Works Agency (UNRWA), responsible

5. "Resolution 194," United Nations Relief and Works Administration (UNRWA) website. https://www.unrwa.org/content/resolution-194.

for Palestinian refugees living in 58 camps across the Middle East. UNRWA continues to operate these camps, providing essential humanitarian services to Palestinian refugees and their descendants. The status of Palestinian refugees today varies from country to country. In Jordan, Palestinian refugees hold Jordanian citizenship. In contrast, Palestinian refugees in Lebanon lead a tightly circumscribed existence, including being barred by law from many professions and from purchasing property.

Israel, for its part, has firmly rejected consideration of Palestinian refugee return. Mainstream Zionism sought to establish a state in which Jews held a demographic majority, a state that could serve as a potential haven for Jews from around the world in the face of anti-Semitism. Allowing Palestinian refugee return would undermine that project. And so, under Israel's Law of Return, Jews from anywhere in the world can move to Israel and become citizens, whereas Palestinians born in what is now Israel who became refugees in 1948 are denied the possibility of return.

The Palestinian national movement was fragmented following the 1948 war—not surprising, given the uprooting of such a large percentage of the Palestinian population during the fighting. While an All-Palestine Government was established in the Egyptian-administered Gaza Strip in September 1948, it had limited powers and was restricted to Gaza. In 1959, a group of Palestinian students and professionals led by Yasser Arafat founded the political movement called Fatah (an Arabic reverse acronym for the Palestinian National Liberation Movement). Fatah eventually joined the Palestine Liberation Organization (PLO), founded in 1964, as the dominant faction. The PLO had as its goal the liberation of Palestine, as an indivisible territorial unit in the boundaries of Mandate Palestine, through armed struggle. For Israel, the PLO's mandate represented a rejectionist denial of its right to exist.

Palestinian Christians played key leadership roles within Fatah and the PLO from its inception—so, for example, a Palestinian from a Christian family uprooted in 1948 from Lydda, George Habash, established the leftist Popular Front for the Liberation of Palestine, one of the PLO's factions.

By the late 1960s, the PLO had widely become recognized among Palestinians as the one legitimate representative of the Palestinian people. The PLO constituted a government in exile, with a legislative body (the Palestinian National Council) and Executive Committee. The PLO also had armed units, while factions within the PLO organized paramilitary wings. The Arab League recognized the PLO as the sole legitimate representative of the Palestinian people at the Rabat Summit in 1974. The PLO's territorial base shifted over the coming decades—first being driven out of Jordan in 1970 following clashes with the Jordanian military (events referred to by Palestinians as Black September), then out of Lebanon during the Israeli invasion of the country in 1982, and finally ending up in Tunisia, until the Oslo Accords brought most of the PLO leadership to the Occupied Territories in 1994.

1967: OCCUPATION BEGINS

If 1948 stands as the most consequential year of the Palestinian-Israeli conflict, 1967 comes a close second. The decade after 1948 witnessed one Arab-Israeli war, as Israel, with support from Great Britain and France, attacked Egypt in the Sinai Peninsula in late 1956 with the goals of securing Western control of the Suez Canal and of removing Egyptian leader Gamal Abdel Nasser from power. After pressure from the United States and the Soviet Union, they withdrew their forces and Nasser remained at Egypt's helm. The June 1967 War, however, proved to be of longer-lasting significance than the Suez War. Historians vigorously debate what and who precipitated the war, but all agree on the final outcome: when fighting ceased, Israel had conquered the Gaza Strip, the West Bank (together with East Jerusalem), the Sinai Peninsula, and the Golan Heights.[6] Israelis refer to the June 1967 War as the Six-Day War; Palestinians, in contrast, refer to it as *an-naksa*, or the setback. Thousands of Palestinians fled and were driven from the West Bank by Israeli forces into Jordan during the course of the fighting, many of them already refugees from 1948.

Less than six months after the fighting ended, the United Nations Security Council (UNSC) adopted Resolution 242, calling for the withdrawal of Israeli troops from territories occupied during the June 1967 war, an end to belligerency, and the recognition of sovereignty by all parties. The UN reiterated this "land-for-peace" principle with UNSC Resolution 338 in 1973, following the October 1973 war between Egypt and Syria, on the one hand, and Israel, on the other, a war that concluded with no change in territorial positions, but that boosted Arab morale following the decisive defeat of the 1967 war. These two resolutions formed the basis of the 1979 Egyptian-Israeli peace agreement (which included an Israeli commitment to return the Sinai Peninsula to Egypt) and the 1994 Jordanian-Israeli peace agreement. UNSC resolutions 242 and 338 have also stood as the international foundations of efforts to resolve the Palestinian-Israeli conflicts through two-state solutions in which a Palestinian nation-state would be established adjacent to Israel in the parts of Mandate Palestine occupied by Israel in 1967.

6. See Appendix 2, Map 3.

Soon after its conquest of the West Bank and the Gaza Strip in June 1967, Israel began building settlements in East Jerusalem. Then, in the 1970s, Israeli settlement construction started to accelerate in the rest of the West Bank, with smaller settlements built in Gaza. Israel routinely used (and continues to use) appeals to security and Ottoman-era land laws allowing the state to seize under-cultivated land in order to justify confiscating Palestinian property, with the confiscated land later used for Israeli Jewish-only settlement construction. Many settlers were motivated by a Kookist-style vision of redeeming the biblical heartland of Judea and Samaria, while others moved to settlements for economic reasons, with housing costs subsidized by the Israeli government. Because international law prevents occupying powers from moving their civilian population into occupied territory, most international law experts and almost all countries in the world consider the settlements to be illegal. Israel, however, views the territories as administered, not occupied, and so argues that settlements are a political matter subject to negotiation, rather than a legal issue.

Israel's military occupation of Palestinian territories poses an existential question for Israel regarding its character. Israel exercises sovereign control in the Occupied Territories. As the sovereign power, Israel has facilitated and encouraged settlement by its Israeli Jewish citizens in the Occupied Territories, yet the millions of Palestinians in the Occupied Territories do not enjoy citizenship rights, but rather live under harsh military rule. Israeli Military Order 101, promulgated shortly after Israel's 1967 conquest, denies Palestinians the right to demonstrate and serves as the legal justification for arresting Palestinians who do so. Meanwhile, Israel draws on British colonial laws as precedent for holding Palestinians in indefinite administrative

detention without charge or trial. Israeli critics of the occupation contend that Israel cannot maintain its claim to be
a democracy while it rules over millions of stateless people.
The discriminatory nature of the two-tiered system of justice in the Occupied Territories, in which Israeli settlers
maintain their full rights as Israeli citizens, while Palestinians are subject to Israeli military rule, becomes harder to
avoid the more that settlements increase and expand and
that Palestinians in the Occupied Territories are confined to
ever more circumscribed parcels of territory disconnected
by walls, militarized fences, checkpoints, and roadblocks.

INTIFADA, THE PEACE PROCESS, AND ITS AFTERMATH

Palestinian resistance entered a new phase in December
of 1987 with the start of the first *intifada* (Arabic for uprising or shaking off) against Israel's military occupation.
Organized and led by Palestinians inside the Occupied Territories, rather than by the PLO leadership in exile, this first
intifada involved widespread, civilian nonviolent actions
including strikes, tax resistance, and more. The following
year, the Palestinian National Council convened in Algeria
to issue a Declaration of Independence, announcing statehood in the 22 percent of Mandate Palestine consisting
of the Occupied Territories. Together with that declaration, the PLO proclaimed its readiness to engage in peace
negotiations with Israel on the basis of UNSC Resolution
242, with an implied readiness to recognize the State of Israel in exchange for Israeli withdrawal from the Occupied
Territories.

The first *intifada* also witnessed the founding of the Islamic Resistance Movement, or Hamas. During the 1970s,
Israel allowed the Gaza branch of the Egyptian Muslim

Brotherhood, led by Sheikh Ahmad Yassin, to develop a network of charitable institutions under the banner of *al-mujamma' al-islamiyya* (the Islamic Gathering), institutions offering health care, education, youth activities, and more, even as Israel actively suppressed civil society organizations it viewed as linked to the PLO. Through this strategy, Israel sought to weaken the secularist PLO and its claim to be the sole, legitimate representative of the Palestinian people. With the founding of Hamas, Palestinian Islamists signaled a shift from a quietist focus on cultivating piety and revived Islamic practice to active resistance aimed at liberating all of historic Palestine as *waqf*, or religious property. Since then, Fatah, as the major faction within the PLO, and Hamas have competed for control over the Palestinian political sphere.

In the early 1990s, peace negotiations between Israel and the Palestinians began. These talks first began as part of a multilateral conference in Madrid, Spain, in the fall of 1991, which in turn led to direct talks between Israel and a joint Jordanian-Palestinian delegation (with Israel publicly refusing to have direct talks with the PLO). In 1993, however, secret talks between Israel and the PLO, facilitated by the Norwegian government, led that September to the first of the so-called Oslo Accords, a Declaration of Principles that laid out the framework for Palestinian self-government in parts of the Occupied Territories. Over the next two years, Israel and the PLO reached a series of additional agreements as part of this Oslo process, agreements that in 1995 led to the establishment of a Palestinian National Authority (PA) in parts of the West Bank and the Gaza Strip. These accords divided up the West Bank into three types of territory—Areas A, B, and C. In Area A, the PA was to exercise autonomy over civilian and (in principle) security affairs; in Area B, the PA would have autonomous responsibility for civilian matters, while Israel retained authority over security; and in Area C, consisting of around 60% of the West Bank, Israel maintained full control.[7]

The Oslo Accords were initially greeted with widespread optimism and celebration among Palestinians in the Occupied Territories. Oslo, however, was not without its detractors. Early critics of the Oslo Accords, such as the Palestinian-American academic Edward Said, described the agreements as a disaster, warning that it would fragment the Palestinian body politic and Palestinian territory while turning the PLO into a subcontractor of Israel's military occupation. The ensuing quarter century, many observers would argue, has borne out these warnings.

The Oslo Accords stipulated a five-year period during which Israel and the PLO would work to achieve agreement on so-called "final status" issues such as permanent borders, the future of Israeli settlements in the Occupied Territories, the status of Palestinian refugees, access to water resources, sovereignty over Jerusalem, and security. The end of this five-year period came and went in 1999, with little progress made on the final status issues and with foundering Israeli-Palestinian relations. The Camp David summit convened by the United States in July 2000 and the ensuing bilateral summit between Israel and the PLO in January 2001 in the Egyptian resort town of Taba represented the last significant negotiations between the two sides, talks that failed to reach agreement on the final status issues. Since then, the peace process has continued in fits and starts (such as when Israeli and Palestinian leaders committed themselves in 2005 to the Road Map for peace developed by the Quartet of the United States, Great Britain, Russia, and the European Union), with both parties proclaiming readiness to engage in negotiations, but also claiming not to find a

7. See Appendix 2, Map 4.

willing partner for such talks. The Arab League, meanwhile, advanced a peace initiative that it reaffirmed in 2007 and 2017, calling for a normalization of relations between Arab states and Israel in exchange for a full Israeli withdrawal from the Occupied Territories and a just resolution of the Palestinian refugee crisis based on UNGA Resolution 194.

By the end of the 1990s, many Palestinians had increasingly come to view the peace process as Israel's diplomatic cover for deepening and expanding the infrastructure of its military occupation. At the end of September 2000, a second *intifada*, often referred to as the *Al-Aqsa intifada*, began, lasting for the next five years. While the second *intifada* included some of the mass nonviolent action that had characterized much of the first *intifada*, it was also marked by greater action on the part of armed Palestinian militias and by suicide bombings. Palestinian resistance, both violent and nonviolent, was met with resounding Israeli military force, as when Israeli troops bombarded and reinvaded Palestinian cities in Area A in the West Bank in 2002. Israel also accelerated a process of unilaterally separating from the Palestinian population centers in the Occupied Territories. Whereas Israel in the 1970s and 1980s had treated the Gaza Strip and the West Bank as a source of inexpensive labor (while also imposing significant limitations on Palestinian economic development), by the 1990s it began severely curtailing the number of work permits it issued to Palestinians from the Occupied Territories. In 2002, Israel began construction on what it terms a "security barrier" and that Palestinians refer to as a "segregation barrier" or an "apartheid wall."[8] This barrier consists of tall concrete walls and networks of militarized fences and patrol tracks snaking deep into the West Bank and in the process creating a *de facto* border that deviates markedly from the 1949

8. See Appendix 2, Map 5.

Armistice Line. Coupled with a network of roadblocks, checkpoints, and Israeli-only roads running through the West Bank, the separation barrier creates what Israeli sociologist Jeff Halper has termed an Israeli "matrix of control" over Palestinians in the Occupied Territories.

Israeli steps of unilateral separation from Palestinians included Israel's 2005 dismantling of its small settlements in the Gaza Strip and the withdrawal of its forces to the borders of the Strip. While this process of what Israel called "disengagement" did mean greater freedom of movement for Palestinians within the Gaza Strip (Israel's small settlements in the Strip and the military zones around them prevented Gazans from accessing much of the Mediterranean coast, while military checkpoints could cut off Palestinian movement between northern and southern Gaza), Israel's unilateral separation from Gaza left Palestinians in the Strip more isolated than ever in what international human rights organizations refer to as the world's largest outdoor prison. Gaza's isolation increased after Hamas's victory in the 2006 Palestinian Legislative Council elections, followed by a deep Hamas-Fatah rift, leaving Hamas controlling the Gaza Strip and Fatah in charge of the West Bank. The tight Israeli economic blockade, coupled with Palestinian political dysfunction, has created a humanitarian crisis in the Gaza Strip, with United Nations observers warning that Gaza will become uninhabitable by 2020.

Many Palestinians and Israelis increasingly despair about the possibility of the peace process reaching agreement on the final status issues. The nearly quarter-century-old peace process, rather than leading to an independent Palestinian state alongside Israel, has gone hand-in-hand with the deepening of Israeli control over and the fragmentation of Palestinian life in the Occupied Territories. Palestinian political fragmentation has accompanied territorial fragmentation. Voices on the Israeli right calling for out-right annexation of the West Bank (while not granting citizenship to Palestinians in the West Bank) grow louder. Meanwhile, some Palestinians and Israelis committed to a peaceful transformation of the conflict question if a two-state solution to the conflict is still viable and dream of alternatives. The current state of the conflict and possible futures will be examined further in chapter 4.

This chapter has narrated the history of the Palestin-ian-Israeli conflict as an asymmetrical conflict between two nationalist projects. One of these projects (Zionism) has proven dominant and ascendant, while the other (Pal-estinian nationalism) is in disarray. The next two chapters examine ways that Christians have sought to understand Zionism, Palestinian dispossession, and prospects for Israeli-Palestinian peace, paying particular attention to Pal-estinian Christian theological analyses. The final chapter will then turn to an assessment of the present state of the conflict and constructive theological reflection about pos-sibilities for the future.

QUESTIONS FOR DISCUSSION

1. When and where did Zionism emerge? What were the conditions within which Zionism arose?

2. What are different types of Zionism? What are key characteristics of each?

3. What territories did Israel occupy in 1967?

4. Name four United Nations resolutions related to the Palestinian-Israeli conflict and identify what they address.

5. How should Christians think about nationalism?

2

PALESTINIAN CHRISTIAN THEOLOGIES OF LAND AND LIBERATION

PALESTINIAN CHRISTIANS, AS OBSERVED in chapter 1, have been active participants in the Palestinian national struggle from the beginning up to the present day. How have Palestinian Christians thought theologically about their situation? What theological assessments have they made of Zionism and the State of Israel? What theologically shaped visions for the future of Palestine and Israel have they articulated? How have they engaged the global church on these matters? This chapter presents an overview of Palestinian Christian theological reflection on these questions, while the following chapter examines how Palestinian Christian theologians have responded to efforts on the part of the global church to think through the connections between

Christian theologies of Judaism, on the one hand, and appraisals of Zionism, on the other.

NARRATIVES OF DISPOSSESSION AND ASSERTION OF PRESENCE

"We belong to the land." This assertion by Elias Chacour, the former Greek Catholic Archbishop for Akko, Haifa, Nazareth, and All Galilee, could be made by any Palestinian Christian theologian. In the face of expulsion, dispossession, and a military occupation regime that leave Palestinians confined to ever more constricted parcels of land, Palestinian Christian theology can in part be understood as a defiant insistence on Palestinians' presence and rightful place in the land. Confronted by a global church that Palestinian Christians often feel is ignorant of or indifferent to their plight, Palestinian Christian theology stands as a demand not to be forgotten. With many Palestinian Christians troubled by the rise of Islamist movements such as Hamas that challenge the secular, pluralist political vision of the PLO and the Palestinian National Authority, Palestinian Christian theologians underscore the church's roots in the land stretching back nearly two thousand years and the place of Christians within the rich diversity of Palestinian society.

Assertions of presence in and belonging to the land go hand-in-hand, for most Palestinian Christian theologians, with narratives of dispossession. Chacour, for example, tells one such *nakba* story from 1948, recounting playing as a boy in his favorite fig tree, planted by his father, when word arrived that the Israeli army would soon be entering his village of Kafr Bir'im in the northern Galilee. Not long thereafter, the Israeli soldiers ordered Chacour and his family, along with their fellow villagers, to evacuate the village, telling them that they would soon be allowed to return. The Bir'imites were kept from returning, with the Israeli military then bombing their homes. The villagers who remained in what became the state of Israel have spent the ensuing decades seeking to return to their land, while the Israeli state built a national park on the village's ruins and turned over village lands to Israeli *kibbutzim* and *moshavim* for their use.

Other Palestinian Christian theologians narrate similar *nakba* stories. The Anglican priest and theologian, Naim Ateek, relates being uprooted as a boy from his native village of Biesan (renamed Bet She'an by Israel) during the 1948 war: Ateek and his family ended up as internally displaced persons in Nazareth. Another Anglican priest, Audeh Rantisi, was also a boy when his family and other Palestinians living in Lydda and Ramle were expelled by Israeli troops (led by future Israeli Prime Minister Yitzhak Rabin) and forcibly sent on a march westward into the Jordanian-controlled West Bank. Quaker theologian Jean Zaru recalls her family opening its land in Ramallah in the West Bank to refugee families. Evangelical pastor Alex Awad relates his family's forced removal from their home in Jerusalem's Musrara neighborhood.

These stories of displacement from the land are not distinctive to Palestinian Christian theologians or to Palestinian Christians. Instead, they echo and reflect the hundreds of thousands of Palestinian stories of forced displacement in 1948 and beyond, stories captured in family and village memory books, oral histories, memorial websites for destroyed villages, and more. By narrating their individual testimonies of dispossession, Palestinian Christian theologians locate their personal experiences and the experiences of Palestinian Christians within the broader story of Palestinian exile from the land. These testimonies of exile, in turn, also serve to reinforce the assertion of the Palestinian people's presence and rightful place in the land. One way to understand Palestinian Christian theology, then, is as an expression of what Palestinians refer to as *sumud*, or steadfastness, amidst forces that would uproot or displace Palestinians. The olive tree stands as a symbol within Palestinian national iconography of such *sumud*. For Palestinian Christians, this arboreal iconography for Palestinian steadfastness echoes God's promise to God's people that "they shall not build and another inhabit; they shall not plant and another eat; for like the days of a tree shall the days of my people be" (Isaiah 65:22).

TYPES OF PALESTINIAN CHRISTIAN THEOLOGY

Christian theology, as talk about God in light of God's incarnation in Jesus, stretches back nearly two thousand years to the days of the early church. Palestinian Christians today claim this ancient tradition as their own. Across Palestine and Israel, Orthodox and Catholic worshippers from diverse communions participate in centuries-old Arabic-, Greek-, Syriac-, Coptic-, Armenian-, and Amharic-language liturgies. When Palestinian Christians today assert their rootedness in the land, they refer in part to this long, unbroken line of Christian worship in the land. So, for example, the twenty Christian families in the northern West Bank village of Burqin proudly point to its Byzantine-era church commemorating Jesus's healing of the ten lepers (Luke 17:11–19) as a testament to their community's long-standing presence in the land.

While significant ecclesial diversity can be found within Palestinian Christianity, most Palestinian Christians belong to one of the three largest Christian communions in Palestine and Israel: the Greek Orthodox, Greek Catholic (or Melkite), and Latin (Roman Catholic) churches. Other Orthodox churches have smaller communities in the Holy Land, including the Armenian Orthodox and the Syrian Orthodox. The Greek Catholic Church, like other Eastern Catholic churches, maintains is own distinctive liturgy and practices, while also in full communion with the Roman Catholic Church. (Eastern Catholic churches have sometimes been called Uniate churches, because of their full communion with Rome—but Eastern Catholic churches themselves reject this label as pejorative.) Protestant Christianity, meanwhile, has a much more recent history in the land, resulting from mission efforts starting in the mid-nineteenth century (with converts to Protestant churches coming almost exclusively from other Christian churches). The Episcopal (Anglican) Diocese of Jerusalem and the Evangelical Lutheran Church of Jordan and the Holy Land are the two officially recognized Protestant churches under the Ottoman-era *status quo* arrangements. These two churches are joined by a variety of other Protestant churches, including evangelical communions.

The mosaic of Christianity in Palestine and Israel is filled out by some non-Palestinian groups. Small groups of Messianic Jews (Jews who follow Jesus, or Yeshua, as the messiah, or *mashiach*) worship across Israel. Messianic Jews often face social discrimination within Israeli society. Most Messianic Jews (both in Israel and globally) are staunchly pro-Zionist. Meanwhile, starting in the 1980s, Israel experienced a wave of immigration from the countries of the former Soviet Union. Some of the new immigrants from these countries, while having Jewish parents or grandparents, arrived self-identifying as Christians and now worship in Messianic Jewish congregations and in Orthodox, Catholic, and other churches. Finally, Christians from countries like the Philippines working as short-term temporary labor inside Israel as well as non-Palestinian clergy and members of religious orders round out the mosaic of Christianity in the land.

Whatever their ecclesial identification, Palestinian Christians take pride in the church's ancient roots in the land. Palestinian Christian theology can thus in part be understood as the enduring worship of God over hundreds of years by churches in the land and the witness of those churches to the good news of humanity's reconciliation to God through Jesus Christ. Palestinian Christian theology is also a recent enterprise, reflecting efforts by Palestinian Christians to think theologically about such matters as land, election, and the Christian call to peacemaking in light of Zionism and Palestinian dispossession.

Palestinian Christians have engaged in such theological reflection since the start of the Palestinian-Israeli conflict through sermons, speeches, poetry, and more, with such reflection shaped by the church's centuries of worship and theological reflection in the land. However, deliberate and sustained theological reflection on Zionism, the *nakba* of 1918, and how those relate to the church's interpretation of Scripture and to its theology of Judaism began to flower in the last quarter of the twentieth century, with self-consciously Palestinian Christian theologizing emerging in the late 1970s and throughout the 1980s.

The blossoming of Palestinian Christian theology during this period can be connected to at least two factors. First, the process of the indigenization of church hierarchies neared completion during this period. Some communions, like the Eastern Catholic and many of the Orthodox churches, have had Arab or other Eastern leadership since their inception. The Latin (Roman Catholic) Church, however, did not have a Palestinian leader until the elevation of Michel Sabbah as Patriarch of Jerusalem

in 1987. Sabbah's appointment followed earlier moves for
the indigenization of ecclesial hierarchies in the two major
Protestant churches in Palestine and Israel, with the Episcopal (Anglican) Diocese of Jerusalem appointing its first
Arab bishop, Najib Cubain, in 1957, and the Evangelical
Lutheran Church of Jordan and the Holy Land consecrat-
ing its first Palestinian bishop, Daoud Haddad, in 1979.
The indigenization of church leadership helped to spur
more sustained attention by the institutional church to its
surrounding context, something that its lay members had
been pressing it to do. These institutional changes, meanwhile, provided fertile ground for the flowering of more
vigorous theological reflection on the Palestinian-Israeli
conflict and the challenges of dispossession and occupation
faced by Palestinians. (While the majority of parish priests
within the Greek Orthodox Church in Palestine and Israel
are Palestinian, the bulk of church's hierarchy comes from
Greece and Cyprus. Palestinian Orthodox laity, however,
have actively pushed for the church to become more outspoken on political matters, often clashing with the church's
hierarchy.)

Second, this blossoming of self-consciously Palestinian Christian theology coincides with the emergence of active civil society organizations in the Occupied Territories
during the late 1970s and into the 1980s. With overt political activity forbidden by the Israeli military authorities, Palestinians in the Occupied Territories turned their political
energies to developing grassroots, community-based organizations addressing a wide variety of matters, from early
childhood education to agricultural development to wom-
en's health and more. Churches also became more active in
social outreach during this period. These bubbling energies
were reflected in the first Palestinian uprising, or *intifada*,
against Israel's military occupation, with its mobilization

of widespread grassroots involvement in resistance efforts. The articulation of distinctively Palestinian theologies reflected this broader period of Palestinian self-assertion.

Palestinians from across the ecumenical spectrum have actively contributed to the development of Palestinian Christian theology over the past three decades. An incomplete listing of Palestinian Christian theologians runs the ecumenical gamut: from Greek Orthodox (Archbishop Theodosios, also known as Atallah Hanna), Armenian Orthodox (lay leader Nora Carmi), Greek Catholic (former Archbishop Elias Chacour and lay leader Geries Khoury), and Roman Catholic (Father Rafiq Khoury and Patriarch Michel Sabbah) to Anglican (Rev. Naim Ateek, lay leader Samia Khoury, and Rev. Audeh Rantisi), Lutheran (Rev. Mitri Raheb and Rev. Munther Isaac), evangelical (pastors Yohanna Katanacho and Alex Awad), and Quaker (Jean Zaru, the presiding clerk of the Ramallah Friends Meeting). The development of Palestinian Christian theology has fostered vigorous and productive conversations across this ecumenical spectrum.

Two main approaches emerged as Palestinian Christian theology began to blossom in the 1980s: *Palestinian liberation theology* and *Palestinian contextual (or local) theology*. Anglican priest Naim Ateek started to lay the groundwork for what he would call a Palestinian liberation theology while serving as a priest in Haifa in the 1970s and then as a doctoral student in San Francisco. Inspired by other efforts to discern theological responses to oppression in Latin American and South Africa and to racism in the United States that underscore God's preferential option for the poor and marginalized, Ateek began to ask what a Palestinian theology of liberation might look like. While serving as Canon of St. George's Cathedral in East Jerusalem, Ateek organized consultations on this question. In 1989,

Ateek laid out his vision for Palestinian liberation theology with his groundbreaking work, *Justice, and Only Justice*. Then, in 1993, Ateek and an ecumenical group of colleagues, including lay women leaders like Cedar Duaybis, Nora Carmi, Samia Khoury, and Violette Khoury, founded the Sabeel Ecumenical Liberation Theology Center. *Sabeel* is an Arabic word meaning both "path" and "spring": one can walk in the *sabeel*, or path, of God, or be refreshed at a life-giving *sabeel*, or spring.

Over the past quarter century, Sabeel has convened ecumenical conversations among Christians across Palestine and Israel, as well as interfaith discussions between Palestinian Christians and Muslims, about what word of hope for liberation faith has to speak into the Palestinian context of dispossession and occupation. Sabeel has also organized regular ecumenical prayer services and Bible studies where Palestinian Christians seek to discern God's path for them and has convened multiple international conferences bringing speakers from around the world for global ecumenical engagement with Palestinian Christians about how Christians should understand Zionism and what faith-shaped peacemaking looks like. Sabeel has also produced a *Contemporary Way of the Cross*, a liturgy for pilgrims that directs people to sites in and around Jerusalem where they can together read Scripture and meditate on the history and ongoing reality of Palestinian dispossession.

In 2000, Sabeel released its *Jerusalem Sabeel Document* outlining what Sabeel views as essential principles for a just Palestinian-Israeli peace. The *Jerusalem Sabeel Document* builds on a theological basis that includes: confession of God as creator and redeemer who loves all people; response to the divine commandment to carry out justice in the land; and an understanding of land as God's good gift that ultimately belongs to God. From this theological basis, the *Jerusalem Sabeel Document* articulates a hope for a solution to the Palestinian-Israeli conflict based on the United Nations Security Council "land-for-peace" resolutions (242 and 338). Sabeel envisions Israeli withdrawal from the Occupied Territories proceeding simultaneously with the establishment of a sovereign and democratic Palestine alongside a sovereign and democratic Israel, with both states sharing Jerusalem. Such a two-state solution to the conflict might in the future then give way to closer connections in a federation, confederation, or one state.

The second major approach within Palestinian Christian theology is local, or contextual, theology. Lutheran priest Mitri Raheb, who undertook his doctoral study in theology in Marburg, Germany, and has pastored for years in Bethlehem, stresses that Palestinians need to develop a contextual theology (*lahut si'aqi* or *lahut mahalli*), one accounting not only for the political realities of dispossession and occupation in which the church finds itself immersed, but also for its cultural context. Through the Diyar Consortium in Bethlehem, Raheb and his colleagues promote Palestinian cultural renewal and a wide variety of Palestinian artistic expression and intellectual production.

Roman Catholic priest Rafiq Khoury has similarly stressed the importance of the cultural context, calling on Palestinian theologians to articulate how the gospel had been incarnated within an "Arab tent." Greek Catholic theologian and erstwhile politician Geries Sa'ed Khoury has also advocated for a Palestinian Christian theology responsive to the local, cultural context, stressing the importance of Christian-Muslim engagement and the affirmation of a shared Christian-Muslim Arab heritage. The two Khourys (no close relation), with support from Michel Sabbah as Latin Patriarch, founded the Al-Liqa' Center in Bethlehem to promote Christian-Muslim conversation and Christian theological reflection on the church's embeddedness in an Arab and overwhelmingly Muslim society. Advocates of contextual theology insist on theological engagement with the surrounding cultural and political context, while emphasizing continuity with the historic teaching of the church universal.

Proponents of these two approaches have advanced constructive critiques of one another.[1] Ateek, for example, suggests that the term "contextual" theology does not specify with enough precision the political context of dispossession and occupation within which Palestinian theologizing unfolds. Proponents of contextual theology and local theology, meanwhile, have critiqued Ateek's liberation theology for not articulating with sufficient care the relationship between liberation and salvation and for being directed toward a European and North American audience, rather than primarily engaging the Palestinian Christian laity. Rafiq Khoury has also observed that the appellation of "liberation theology" evoked Latin America, a context in which Christians comprise the majority. A Palestinian Christian theology that seeks to think about the meaning of liberation within the context of dispossession and occupation, Khoury contends, must also account for the fact that Christians in Palestine (as throughout the Middle East) are part of a mainly Islamic milieu.

The differences between these two broad approaches within Palestinian Christian theology should not be overstated, however. Ateek has regularly invited contextual theologians to speak at international conferences organized by Sabeel. Rafiq Khoury and Geries Khoury, meanwhile, have included Ateek in study conferences held by the Al-Liqa' Center. Contextual theologians also concur that the

1. For a longer examination of the types of Palestinian Christian theology, see Gräbe, *Kontextuelle palästinensische Theologie*.

struggle for liberation from dispossession and occupation is an essential part of the local context that contextual theologies must address.

While churches in Palestine and Israel, like churches in other parts of the world, are no strangers to theological disagreement (conflicts historically exacerbated in the Holy Land due to tensions over control of Christianity's holy sites), the Jerusalem Heads of Churches have helped shape an ecumenical agenda that confronts and responds to Israel's military occupation. Since 1988 (shortly after the start of the first *intifada*), the Jerusalem Heads of Churches—representing the Orthodox, Catholic, and Protestant churches recognized under the Ottoman-era *status quo*—have jointly issued scores of declarations, statements, and pastoral letters responding to political developments. Melanie May has gathered 68 of these statements, released between 1988 and 2008, in her book, *Jerusalem Testament*. Some of these ecumenical statements are pastorally-focused, directed to the Palestinian faithful, while others advocate to political leaders that they direct their energies and power towards the promotion of justice and peace for all in the land of Palestine and Israel.

The past three decades have also witnessed accelerated ecumenical cooperation among Palestinian Christians at the grassroots level in discerning the proper Christian response to occupation, *intifada*, and the construction of physical walls and barriers that divide Palestinians from Palestinians as well as Palestinians from Israelis. The culmination of this ecumenical work has been the *Kairos Palestine Document*, penned in 2009 by an inter-confessional group of laity and clergy and affirmed by the Jerusalem Heads of Churches. This ecumenical document, discussed in greater detail at the end of this chapter, offers a shared Palestinian Christian vision for the future and issues a call to the church worldwide to stand in solidarity with the Palestinian church.

KEY THEMES IN PALESTINIAN CHRISTIAN THEOLOGIES

A short study such as this cannot adequately convey the full nuances and richness of the varied arguments and proposals advanced by Palestinian Christian theologians. This book is therefore no substitute for actually reading what Palestinian Christian theologians have written. The Further Reading section at the end of this book lists some of the most important works of Palestinian Christian theology.

While Palestinian Christian theologies are diverse and have differing emphases, a review of these theologies uncovers some common themes and shared questions with which Palestinian Christian theologians grapple. All Palestinian Christian theologians seek to counter theological justifications for Zionism and Palestinian dispossession. As they do so, these Palestinian Christian thinkers develop theological accounts of election, land, and the church's mission in the midst of conflict.

Election and God's Promises

Palestinian Christian theologians object to theologies that conflate the biblical people of Israel with the modern State of Israel. Such theologies contend that the biblical land promises to Abraham and his descendants provide justification for the modern Zionist project of establishing Jewish control over the land. In so doing, these theologians provide justification for Palestinian dispossession.

Theological justifications of Zionism (including Christian Zionism, to be examined more closely in chapter

3 below) maintain that God's covenantal bond with the Jewish people is unbroken and conclude from that premise that God's promises of the land to the people of Israel remain valid. For Christian Zionists, God's promise to Abram that "I will bless those who bless you, and the one who curses you I will curse" (Genesis 12:3) calls Christians today to support Israel. Similarly, praying for the peace of Jerusalem (Psalm 122:6) means praying for and acting in support of the State of Israel.

Palestinian Christian theologians respond to theologies that link God's election of the people of Israel to justifications of Zionism in multiple ways. First, they insist that Christian interpretation of Scripture must start and end with God's incarnation and self-revelation in Jesus Christ. God's promises to the people of Israel in the Old Testament, or Hebrew Bible, have been fulfilled in Jesus, God's chosen one. Second, Palestinian Christian theologians contend that God's election of the people of Israel was for a universal, not exclusive, mission, a mission of calling all of humanity back to its creation in God's image (Genesis 1:27). All peoples share in the *imago Dei*, or image of God—accordingly, all peoples bear rights and dignity that must not be violated by oppressive systems that exclude. The world is blessed through Abraham and his descendants because their story opens out onto a universal mission of sharing God's love for the entire world (John 3:16) and the ingrafting of Gentiles into the vine of God's love (Romans 9–11). The example of the reluctant prophet Jonah reveals the wideness of God's love and mercy, with Jonah's exclusivist chauvinism upended by God's love for the people of Nineveh. While Palestinian Christian theologians join the global church in grappling with what it would mean to confess that God remains in covenant relationship with the Jewish people after the fulfillment of biblical promises in Jesus Christ (to be explored further in chapter 3), they emphasize that God's election of the people of Israel was ultimately for inclusive, rather than exclusive, purposes.

Theology of Land

Palestinian Christian theologians, mirroring biblical theologians like Walter Brueggemann and Norman Habel, recognize that there are multiple theologies of the land operating within Scripture. One strand of biblical land theology bears disquieting resonances for Palestinian Christians. Palestinians remembering homes, fields, and trees lost during the *nakba* or confiscated as part of Israel's military occupation find disturbing parallels in the conquest theology in which God talks of giving the Israelites "a land with fine, large cities that you did not build, houses filled with all sorts of goods that you did not fill, hewn cisterns that you did not hew, vineyards and olive groves that you did not plant" (Deuteronomy 6:10–11; see also Joshua 24:13).

To counter such conquest theology, Palestinian Christian theologians highlight other strands of biblical land theology. One such strand emphasized by Palestinian Christian theologians is the repeated emphasis across the Hebrew scriptures that the land ultimately belongs to God and that the people of Israel in the land are thus not masters in the land. God repeatedly admonishes the Israelites to remember that they were once foreigners in Egypt and so must not mistreat foreigners in their midst (Exodus 22:21, Deuteronomy 10:19, Leviticus 19:34). Yet, as God reminds the Israelites, they remain aliens even in the land of Israel. So, for example, in the course of commanding the Israelites to observe a Jubilee every fifty years of release for the land and the people in it, God declares that "the land is mine; with me you are but aliens and tenants" (Leviticus

25:23). Palestinian Christian theologies thus proceed from the starting point that the land is not the exclusive possession of any one people or group, but rather belongs to God. Land is a good gift from God that ultimately remains God's possession.

Palestinians and Israelis must therefore act as faithful stewards of this good gift of land, Palestinian Christian theologians maintain. Being good stewards means acting justly in the land. In fact, Palestinian Christian theologians emphasize, the land vomits out those who fail to act justly (Leviticus 18:25).

The Church's Cry for Justice and Its Mission of Peacemaking and Reconciliation

Several Palestinian Christian theologians draw parallels between the Roman occupation of the land of Israel in Jesus's day and present-day Israel's military occupation. Just as the prophet Elijah denounced the murder of the farmer Naboth, arranged by Queen Jezebel so that King Ahab might take possession of Naboth's vineyard (1 Kings 21), so do Palestinian Christian theologians denounce Israeli measures that dispossess Palestinians. In the face of occupation and empire, these theologians contend, God's people cry out for justice, while also working for peace and reconciliation. Palestinian Christian theologies are animated by hope for the day in which God's "justice will dwell in the wilderness and righteousness in the fruited field" (Isaiah 32:16–18). Justice is the foundation of peace: establishing justice leads to peace and security.

Doing justice, however, must be wedded to merciful kindness and humility (Micah 6:8). While few Palestinian Christians subscribe to a strict pacifism, a striking characteristic shared by Palestinian Christian theologies is an emphasis on nonviolent, as opposed to armed, struggle. This commitment to nonviolent resistance flows in part from a pragmatic appraisal of the futility of armed struggle against a heavily armed Israeli opponent. More fundamentally, however, the embrace of nonviolence is grounded in the theological conviction that Christians and the church are called by Christ to be peacemakers and by the confession of a God who acts through Christ to tear down walls of hostility that divide (Ephesians 2:10–20).

This theological insistence on nonviolence also reflects the fact that Palestinian Christians have played leading roles in promoting nonviolent direct action. So, for example, during the first *intifada* the Christian community of Beit Sahour in the West Bank mobilized city-wide tax resistance, organized strikes, and established a clandestine dairy operation in an attempt to avoid dependency on Israeli dairy products: the animated movie, *The Wanted 18*, offers a humorous account of how the residents of Beit Sahour hid their dairy cows from Israeli military forces seeking to close down this unlicensed milk operation.

Role of the Church within Palestinian Society

While Christians represent a small percentage of the Palestinian population inside Israel and the Occupied Territories, Palestinian Christian theologians, like Palestinian Christians generally, resist being called a minority. Palestinian Christians recognize, of course, that numerically they represent a much smaller part of Palestinian society than do Palestinian Muslims. Objections to the term minority are not a denial of demographic facts, but rather reflect an insistence that Christians have been and continue to be an integral part of Palestinian society, rather than a separate group. British colonial authorities in Mandate Palestine sought to deploy the divide-and-rule strategies the British empire had used elsewhere; the Israeli state has continued this colonial tactic of seeking to divide the indigenous population. In the face of such tactics, Palestinian Christian theologians insist that Christians are indivisible from the broader Palestinian people.

Palestinian Christian theologians underscore the distinctive ministry and witness of peacemaking and reconciliation the church has to play within the broader Palestinian society. Emigration of Christians from Palestine and Israel represents a grave concern for Palestinian church leaders. If Palestinian Christians, frustrated by the economic and political uncertainty wrought by the Israeli military occupation and by discriminatory laws and policies inside Israel, continue to emigrate, this particular vocation of the church in Palestine and Israel is threatened. The percentage of Christians among the Palestinian population in Palestine has steadily declined over the course of the twentieth century up to the present, down from 10–15 percent at the start of the 1900s to 2 percent today. Multiple factors account for this decrease. Palestinian Christians, like Palestinian Muslims, faced displacement in 1948 and 1967. Like their counterparts within the Palestinian Muslim community, middle-class Palestinian Christians with resources and connections have sought to escape the constricted possibilities and daily degradations of life under occupation by seeking education, security, and economic opportunities outside of Palestine and Israel. These factors, coupled with a lower overall birthrate for Palestinian Christians compared to Palestinian Muslims, have contributed to the downward trend in the overall percentage of Christians within Palestinian society.

In the face of the threats posed by such emigration, Palestinian Christian theologians and church leaders call on the global church to show solidarity with the Palestinian church. Hundreds of thousands of Christian pilgrims each year visit Palestine and Israel, praying at holy sites such as the Church of the Holy Sepulcher in Jerusalem and the Church of the Nativity in Bethlehem. For Palestinian Christians, these and other churches are regular places of worship. Palestinian Christian theologians stress that Christians in Palestine and Israel are the "fifth Gospel" as well as "living stones" (1 Peter 2:5). Palestinian Christian leaders call on Christian pilgrims not only to visit the stones of centuries-old churches, but also to engage the living stones who worship within those church buildings.

KAIROS PALESTINE AND VISIONS OF RECONCILIATION IN THE LAND

Many of the themes running through Palestinian Christian theologies come together in the 2009 *Kairos Palestine Document*, officially titled *A Moment of Truth: A Word of Faith, Hope, and Love from the Heart of Palestinian Suffering.* This document, composed by a group of fifteen men and women representing the wide array of Palestinian ecclesial communions, represents a major milestone in Palestinian Christian theology. The drafting committee for the *Kairos Palestine Document* included prominent Palestinian theologians and clergy from across the ecumenical spectrum (from Greek Orthodox, Greek Catholic, and Roman Catholic to Anglican, Lutheran, and evangelical) and included three Palestinian lay women: Lucy Talgieh (Roman Catholic), Cedar Duaybis (Anglican), and Nora Kort (Greek Orthodox).

The *Kairos Palestine Document* modeled itself on the *Kairos Document* issued in 1985 by a group of primarily black South African church leaders and theologians condemning their country's discriminatory apartheid regime while also critiquing a "church theology" that promoted quietism and advocating for a "prophetic theology" that speaks a word of liberation amid oppression.

Like Palestinian Christian theology generally, the *Kairos Palestine Document* affirms the rightful place of Palestinians in the land, underscoring their deep history in and connections to the land. Theologies like Christian Zionism that would deny Palestinians' place in the land or justify their dispossession are therefore to be rejected. Such theologies distort the good, life-giving news of the gospel for all into a sign of death for Palestinians.

As a counter to theologies that exclusively restrict God's promises and deny Palestinians a place in the land, the *Kairos Palestine Document* advances a theology that starts with the dignity of all human beings as creatures made in God's image. Any political arrangements in the land must safeguard and protect that dignity. The occupation "distorts the image of God in the Israeli who has become an occupier just as it distorts this image in the Palestinian living under occupation."[2]

The land, the writers insist, ultimately belongs to God (Psalm 24:1). As such, the land has a "universal mission," a mission in which "the meaning of the promises, of the land, of the election, of the people of God open up to include all of humanity, starting from all the peoples of this land." God's promise of the land, the writers continue, "has never been a political programme, but rather the prelude to complete universal salvation. It was the initiation of the fulfilment of the Kingdom of God on earth."[3] Recognition that the land belongs to God calls the Jews, Christians, and Muslims who live in the land "to respect the will of God" for the land by liberating the land from "the evil of injustice

2. Kairos Palestine, *A Moment of Truth*, 2.5.

3. Ibid., 2.3.

and war." Because the land is God's land, it must become "a land of reconciliation, peace, and love."[4]

The *Kairos Palestine Document* pays close attention to the distinctive vocation of the Palestinian church. The church's mission in the midst of injustice and occupation is "to proclaim the Kingdom of God, a kingdom of justice, peace and dignity." The vocation of the Palestinian church "is to bear witness to the goodness of God and the dignity of human beings." The church's call is "to pray and to make our voice heard when we announce a new society where human beings believe in their own dignity and the dignity of their adversaries."[5] Because "the Kingdom of God on earth is not dependent on any political orientation," being "greater and more inclusive than any particular political system," the church must "promote justice, truth and human dignity."[6] Christians should advocate and struggle for polities free from "discrimination and exclusion" and the rule of "one citizen over another."[7] In the face of military occupation and systems of discrimination, Christians have a duty to resist. This resistance, however, must be "creative resistance" that "engages the humanity of the enemy." Resistance against oppression must be conformed to Christ's example and must thus operate not through death-dealing but through love.[8]

Kairos Palestine also includes a message for the global church. In addition to expressing gratitude for ecumenical fellowship and solidarity, the *Kairos Palestine Document* calls on churches to repent of pro-Zionist theologies that deny Palestinians a rightful place in the land. The global

4. Ibid., 2.3.1.
5. Ibid., 3.4.2.
6. Ibid., 3.4.3.
7. Ibid., 9.3,
8. Ibid., 4.2.

church must "preserve the word of God as good news for all rather than to turn it into a weapon with which to slay the oppressed." Christians from around the world are invited to "come and see" the realities facing the church in the land. Churches around the world are also urged to consider non-violent methods, including boycotts and divestment, for promoting "justice, peace, and security for all."[9]

Some churches in the United States and beyond have responded positively to these calls from Kairos Palestine, including pursuing efforts to divest financial resources from support for Israel's military occupation. Others have condemned Kairos Palestine for failing, from their perspective, to recognize the special role that Zionism and the State of Israel have to play within God's providential plan for the world. Still others, meanwhile, grapple with how to receive Kairos Palestine's call while also repenting of the church's sordid history of anti-Semitism and while maintaining the church's newfound appreciation for God's enduring, covenantal faithfulness to the Jewish people. The next chapter will explore how Christian theologies of Judaism have shaped understandings of Zionism and the State of Israel and examine how Palestinian Christian theologians have engaged and critiqued those theologies.

QUESTIONS FOR DISCUSSION

1. Why are personal narratives a significant part of Palestinian Christian theologies? How have personal, family, and community stories shaped your theological perspectives?

2. When does contemporary Palestinian Christian theology emerge? What were other trends in Palestinian

9. Ibid., 6.

society and within Palestinian churches at this time?

3. What are two main approaches within Palestinian Christian theology? What are their distinctive emphases? What critiques do theologians representing these two approaches have of the other approach?

4. What are some scriptural themes about land highlighted by Palestinian Christian theologians?

5. Why do Palestinian Christians resist being described as a minority community?

6. What are particular actions to which the *Kairos Palestine Document* calls the global church?

3

CHRISTIAN THEOLOGIES OF JUDAISM AND ASSESSMENTS OF ZIONISM

While the last chapter focused specifically on how Palestinian Christians have reflected theologically about the Palestinian-Israeli conflict, this chapter uses a broader lens to consider how Christians globally have approached Zionism. The chapter begins with an overview of Christian Zionism (from its origins in the late sixteenth and early seventeenth century to its influence on Puritanism to its present-day global reach and staunch advocacy for policies on the far right of the Israeli political spectrum), followed by a consideration of Palestinian Christian objections to Christian Zionism.

The focus then shifts to an analysis of how, following World War II and the revelation of the brutal devastation of the Holocaust, Catholic and Protestant churches undertook theological introspection about histories of anti-Semitism and started reviewing, revising, and discarding teachings of contempt for or replacement of the Jewish people. This revisionary work included affirmation of God's enduring covenantal relationship with the Jewish people. For some, this affirmation in turn entailed the ongoing legitimacy of biblical land promises, thus providing justification for the Zionist enterprise. For others, confession of Christian histories of anti-Semitism in the wake of the Holocaust demanded action to ensure Jewish security, which in turn required defense of the State of Israel as a secure home for the Jewish people.

The chapter concludes with a case study of how one Palestinian Christian theologian, Roman Catholic leader Michel Sabbah, thinks about the interrelationship between election and land promises. While claims to being God's chosen people have often underwritten exclusionary land claims and projects of dispossession, Sabbah counters that God elects people and individuals for a vocation of witnessing to God's universal love for all. Sabbah in turn argues that the universal vocation of God's chosen people must nurture a forceful critique of any political system built on exclusion and oppression and a vision for a shared future based on recognition of the dignity shared by Palestinians and Israelis as creatures made in God's image.

CHRISTIAN ZIONISM

Christian Zionism refers here to Christian support for the return of Jews to the biblical land of Israel linked to eschatological hopes regarding the fulfillment and end of history. Christian Zionism has become a significant political force over the past several decades. Its roots, however, can be traced back to the late 1500s and to restorationist theologies (which, as the name suggests, hoped and prayed for the restoration of the Jewish people to the land). While Christian Zionists today disagree amongst themselves on points of biblical interpretation, understandings of the end times, and the question of missionary efforts to Jews, they agree that support for Zionism and the State of Israel is an urgent Christian duty and that God will bless those who support the State of Israel and the Jewish people.

Already in the late sixteenth century, Thomas Brightman, an Anglican clergyman and author of an influential commentary on the Book of Revelation, interpreted biblical prophecy as foretelling the coming restoration of the Jewish people to the land. A Judeocentric approach to biblical prophecy that interpreted the Bible as prophesying such restoration gained traction among other Anglican clergy as the seventeenth century progressed. Christian Zionism in the United States today, meanwhile, has roots reaching back to the Puritans.

With the rise of European nationalism in the 1800s, the restorationist theologies that had percolated in the United Kingdom, the United States, and beyond began to assume political dimensions as well. In the mid-nineteenth century, the 7th Earl of Shaftesbury, Lord Anthony Ashley-Cooper, an active proponent of Christian mission to Jews, became an ardent advocate to the British government that it should work to facilitate Jewish restoration to the land. In the United States, meanwhile, real-estate developer William Blackstone, whose 1878 book, *Jesus is Coming*, sold millions of copies, rallied religious and business leaders to support Jewish return to Palestine. In 1890, Blackstone organized a petition (which came to be known as the Blackstone

Memorial) to then-U.S. President Benjamin Harrison asking for U.S. support for Jewish restoration to the land. The petition was signed by over 400 religious leaders, heads of industry, and politicians. In the late 1890s, Anglican Restorationist clergyman William Hechler befriended Theodor Herzl and worked to introduce him to Christian leaders committed to Jewish return to the land.

The restorationist stream of Christian theology was internally diverse, as is Christian Zionist theology today. Proponents of Jewish restoration to the land have differed over eschatology and on Christian mission to the Jewish people. Some Christian Zionists and their restorationist predecessors have actively supported Christian evangelism efforts to the Jewish people, while others have been indifferent, or even opposed to, such efforts. Regarding eschatology, Christian Zionists have disagreed about how to interpret the Book of Revelation's reference to a thousand year rule of the faithful while Satan is bound: for premillennialists, this thousand year reign will begin with Christ's Second Coming, while for postmillennialists, Christ's return will come at the end of this millennial period.

One form of premillennialist fervor for Jewish restoration to the land was represented by the British theologian, John Nelson Darby, whose work was popularized within American fundamentalism in the early twentieth century by C. I. Scofield's Reference Bible. Darby divided the history of God's interaction with humanity into different "dispensations," with the final dispensation being the millennial reign of Christ on earth and with Jewish return to the land an indispensable part of the divine fulfillment of history. Premillennial dispensationalism has greatly influenced Christian Zionist thought. That said, many oppose it, rooting their pro-Zionist convictions instead in God's enduring covenantal promises to God's people. The International

Christian Embassy of Jerusalem (ICEJ), for example, is a prominent example of non-dispensationalist Christian Zionism.

Over the decades, Christian Zionist theology has been further popularized in a variety of Christian pop-culture manifestations, from Hal Lindsey's 1970 best-selling treatise, *The Late Great Planet Earth*, to the *Left Behind* novels (and related movies, video games, and other paraphernalia) from the mid-1990s to the early 2000s. Christian Zionism has developed a worldwide reach through mission efforts and global Christian networks. The blue-and-white Israeli flag with the Star of David can be found prominently displayed in many evangelical sanctuaries across Latin America, Africa, and Asia.

Meanwhile, Christian Zionist theologies animate active political lobbies on behalf of the most extreme positions on the Israeli political spectrum. In the United States, Christian Zionist political advocacy and engagement take a variety of forms, from the idiosyncratic to the highly mobilized, from grassroots congregational action to efficient lobbying organizations on Capitol Hill. Some examples include:

- Congregations "adopting" or "sponsoring" Israeli settlements in the Occupied Territories.

- Every year during the Feast of Tabernacles, the ICEJ hosts a massive rally in Jerusalem of Christian Zionists from all parts of the world to "bless Israel."

- Members of far-right Israeli political parties, including proponents of the "transfer" (i.e., expulsion) of Palestinians from the land, are regular speakers at Christian Zionist conferences.

- A rancher in Texas has tried to breed the red heifer whose ashes would be required for the purification rituals necessary for the inauguration of the Third Temple, which Jewish and Christian extremists hope to have re-established in place of the Dome of the Rock and the Al-Aqsa Mosque.

- Televangelist Pat Robertson has threatened that Christian Zionists would start a third party were a Republican administration to pressure Israel to share Jerusalem.

- Through lobbying organizations such as John Hagee's Christians United for Israel, Christian Zionists organize prayer vigils and letter writing campaigns in support of Israeli military offensives and against any Israeli territorial concessions.

Many Messianic Jews (Jewish followers of Jesus, or Yeshua), both in Israel and globally, are ardent supporters of Zionism. While Messianic Jews disagree with one another on a variety of theological matters, many would share Christian Zionism's linkage of the founding of the State of Israel with eschatological expectations.

PALESTINIAN CHRISTIANS RESPOND TO CHRISTIAN ZIONISM

For Palestinian Christians, Christian Zionism represents a heretical distortion of the good news of God's love for all people. In Christian Zionist theologies, Palestinian theologians argue, Palestinians simply drop off the moral radar screen, at best ignored and at worst viewed as obstacles to God's will that must be removed in order for Jewish restoration to the land to unfold.

Alex Awad of the Bethlehem Bible College relates an incident at a meeting of Palestinian evangelical leaders in

Bethlehem that illustrates Christian Zionist logic taken to an extreme:

> An American woman who was present at the meeting approached one of the pastors and asked him if she could say a few words to the assembly. The pastor, desiring to show courtesy to the guest, asked the emcee (also a Palestinian pastor) if the lady could say her few words. The emcee, unaware of what was coming, agreed to let her talk. When the lady took the microphone, I couldn't believe the words that came out of her mouth. She professed to the Palestinian Evangelical Christians assembled there that she had a word from the Lord for them. "God," she said, "wanted them all to leave Israel and go to other Arab countries." She added that they must leave to make room for God's chosen people, the Jews. She warned the pastors and the audience that if they did not listen to the instructions which God had given her, God would pour his wrath on them.[1]

In August 2006, a group of Palestinian church leaders, led by the Latin (Roman Catholic) Patriarch of Jerusalem and the Holy Land, Michel Sabbah, issued the *Jerusalem Declaration on Christian Zionism*. These church leaders categorically rejected "Christian Zionist doctrines as false teaching that corrupts the biblical message of love, justice and reconciliation." Christian Zionism rests on a faulty eschatology, they argued. They explained further that "We reject the teachings of Christian Zionism that facilitate and support [discriminatory Israeli policies] as they advance racial exclusivity and perpetual war rather than the gospel of universal love, redemption and reconciliation taught by

1. Awad, "Christian Zionism," 2.

Jesus Christ." Instead, they continued, Christians must insist on respect for human dignity based on the creation of all human beings—Israelis as well as Palestinians—in the image of God.[2]

POST-HOLOCAUST CHRISTIAN THEOLOGIES OF JUDAISM AND ASSESSMENTS OF ZIONISM

While the decades following the establishment of the State of Israel witnessed a revival of Christian eschatological hopes linked to Jewish return to the land, these post-Holocaust years also saw the start of Christian self-examination regarding Christianity's legacies of anti-Semitism and anti-Jewish theology. So, for example, church leaders gathered at the founding assembly of the World Council of Churches (WCC) in Amsterdam in 1948 called on churches to "denounce anti-Semitism, no matter what its origin, as absolutely irreconcilable with the profession and practice of the Christian faith." Anti-Semitism, the assembly insisted, "is a sin against God"[3] Then, at the global ecumenical body's third assembly in 1961 in New Delhi, the WCC rejected theologies that attributed collective guilt to Jews for Jesus's death, arguing that Christian teaching should not present "the historic events which led to the Crucifixion" in a manner "as to impose upon the Jewish people of today responsibilities which must fall on all humanity, not on one race or community."[4]

Catholic leaders at the Second Vatican Council (commonly referred to as Vatican II) in 1965 made similar

2. "Palestinian Church Leaders' Statement on Christian Zionism," 211.

3. World Council of Churches, "The Christian Approach to the Jews."

4. World Council of Churches, "Resolution on Anti-Semitism."

theological moves in one of the council's key documents, the Declaration of the Relation of the Church to Non-Christian Religions, or *Nostra Aetate*. In the section on the church's relationship to Judaism, *Nostra Aetate* deplored "all hatreds, persecutions, displays of anti-Semitism directed against the Jews at any time or from any source." The declaration also opposed theologies that attributed to Jews collective guilt for Jesus's death, stressing that "neither all Jews indiscriminately [in Jesus's day], nor Jews today, can be charged with the crimes committed during [Jesus's] passion." It continued that while "the church is the new people of God," the Jewish people "should not be spoken of as rejected or accursed."[5]

The past seventy years have witnessed a flowering of Christian-Jewish dialogue, Christian research into and repentance for histories of anti-Semitism and anti-Judaism, recovery and renewed appreciation for Christianity's Jewish roots, and Christian theological reflection on what it means and does not mean to confess that God's promises to the people first called Israel have been fulfilled in Jesus Christ. Franklin Sherman has collected scores of statements, resolutions, and encyclicals representing these decades of renewed Christian theological engagement with Judaism. These documents reflect the growing conviction within Catholic and Protestant theology over these decades that the fulfillment of God's promises in Jesus Christ does not mean the breaking of God's covenant with the Jewish people.[6]

A survey of these widely diverse documents uncovers a diversity of approaches to how Christians should think about Zionism and the State of Israel. Some statements

5. Pope Paul VI, *Nostra Aetate*, 4.

6. See Sherman, *Bridges: Documents of the Christian-Jewish Dialogue* (2 volumes).

simply ignore or bracket discussion of Zionism. Others emphasize the need for the State of Israel's security, while sometimes, but not always, also addressing Palestinian needs and aspirations. And still others see in Zionism and in Jewish return to the land a mysterious sign of God's covenantal faithfulness. Unlike the Christian Zionist theologies discussed above, these Protestant and Catholic affirmations of Zionism are not tied to an eschatological vision of history's consummation.

Free-church historian Franklin Littel and Episcopalian theologian Paul Van Buren are examples of Christian championing of Zionism not linked to eschatological schema. Both theologians saw in Zionism and the establishment of the modern nation-state of Israel positive, if mysterious, signs of God's covenantal faithfulness to the Jewish people. Littel, for example, described the birth of the Israeli state as a resurrection of Judaism following its crucifixion over centuries of anti-Jewish violence, with the Holocaust as the most horrific example. Christians should recognize God at work in the establishment of the Jewish state, he asserted. "The restitution of Israel," according to Littel, "is the event which challenges Christians to take events, history, and the world seriously again." Therefore, "no one can be an enemy of Zionism and be a friend of the Jewish people today"; to be opposed to Zionism means being opposed to God's work to restore the Jewish people to their land.[7]

Van Buren similarly interprets the creation of the State of Israel as the fulfillment of the land promises in the still-operative, unbroken covenant between God and the Jewish people. Because "landed life, as Israel testifies to it, entails having political control over that land," the establishment of the modern nation-state of Israel represents a necessary dimension of the outworking of God's promise of the land.

7. Littel, *Crucifixion of the Jewish People*, 96–97.

"Israel belongs in *eretz yisrael* free of foreign domination," Van Buren claims. "The realization of this central Jewish hope, under contemporary conditions, requires the state of Israel." Van Buren then proceeds to conclude that "anti-Zionism therefore is in fact an anti-Jewish position."[8]

A 2004 statement from a Catholic-Jewish dialogue repeats this connection between a revised theology of Judaism, on the one hand, and a rejection of anti-Zionism, on the other. The participants at the 18th International Catholic-Jewish Liaison Committee Meeting held in Buenos Aires in July of that year equated anti-Zionism with anti-Semitism and linked that equation with the theological affirmation of God's abiding covenant with the Jewish people. "We draw encouragement from the fruits of our collective strivings which include the recognition of the unique and unbroken covenantal relationship between God and the Jewish People and the total rejection of anti-Semitism in all its forms, including anti-Zionism as a more recent manifestation of anti-Semitism," the concluding conference statement declared. Anti-Zionism is thus collapsed into anti-Semitism from this perspective, to be rejected by Christians who recognize "the unique and unbroken covenantal relationship between God and the Jewish people."[9]

CASE STUDY: MICHEL SABBAH ON ELECTION, LAND, AND THE STATE OF ISRAEL

Palestinian Christian theologians have responded to global Christian efforts to revise Christian theologies of Judaism with skepticism. First, Palestinian Christians rightly observe that they have largely been missing from Jewish-Christian

8. Van Buren, *A Christian Theology of the People Israel*, 199–200.

9. *Joint Declaration of the 18th International Catholic-Jewish Liaison Meeting*.

dialogues and that such dialogues thus often do not address how Jews and Christians understand Zionism and the State of Israel or, if they do, fail to incorporate Palestinian Christian voices. Second, many Palestinian Christian theologians note that revised Christian theologies of Judaism have often been intertwined with theological defenses of Zionism. To affirm that God remains in covenant relationship with the Jewish people, they worry, inevitably leads to an affirmation that biblical land promises to the Jewish people remain valid and in turn to theological justifications of Zionism (and thus of Palestinian dispossession).

Palestinian evangelical theologian Alex Awad is representative of Palestinian Christian worries about how revised theologies of Judaism are often enmeshed with theological justifications of Zionism. Against theological affirmations of God's enduring covenant with the Jewish people, Awad argues that to claim that God's covenant with the Jewish people has not come to an end is to "promote an additional plan for the Jews"—and this move, Awad contends, leads to viewing Palestinian dispossession as inevitable and justifiable as part of God's plan for the Jewish people. To argue that God maintains a particular covenant with the Jewish people distinct from God's covenant with all of humanity through Jesus Christ, Awad believes, contradicts "the core message of the New Testament": "To have a special plan for the Jews or any other race is to diminish the power and the effect of the salvation that God has provided for all people by the death of Jesus Christ on the cross."[10]

How to understand election and biblical land promises without theologically justifying the uprooting of the Palestinian people? Michel Sabbah tackled this question in his pastoral letters during his more than two decades spent serving as the Latin Patriarch of Jerusalem (that is, as the

10. Awad, *Palestinian Memories,* 265–66.

head of the Roman Catholic Church in the Holy Land). After a brief examination of Sabbah's personal history and the
significance of his becoming the first Palestinian to serve as
Latin Patriarch, focus shifts to an examination of Sabbah's
treatment of election and land promises.

Sabbah shares with the majority of Palestinians a story
of displacement and exile. Born in 1933 in Nazareth, Sabbah was a student at the Latin Patriarchate's seminary in Beit
Jala (a few kilometers from Bethlehem) in 1948 when the
war cut him off from his family: Nazareth was now in the
newly created State of Israel, while Sabbah found himself
in the Jordanian-controlled West Bank. As a result, Sabbah
was unable to attend his father's funeral in 1957. After being
ordained and completing a doctorate in Arabic language
and literature at the Sorbonne, Sabbah proceeded to serve
in parishes in Jordan for the next three decades. However,
because he happened by chance to be in East Jerusalem on
church business in June of 1967 when Israel conquered the
West Bank, Sabbah received an Israeli-issued Jerusalem ID
card, making travel to Israel to visit his family and the city
of his birth possible once more.

Sabbah was appointed Latin Patriarch of Jerusalem in
1987, a position he held until 2008. Since stepping down as
Patriarch, Sabbah has been a leading figure in the Kairos
Palestine movement (discussed in chapter 2). Sabbah's appointment as Patriarch coincided with the start of the first
Palestinian *intifada* against Israeli military occupation.
Shortly after assuming the position of Patriarch, Sabbah
moved to curtail interactions with Israeli authorities to a
minimum and, in accordance with the directives of the
Unified National Leadership of the *intifada*, cancelled all of
the celebratory processions associated with major Christian
feast days (e.g., Christmas, Palm Sunday, Easter), observing
only the liturgical ceremonies. Israeli officials responded by

routinely accusing Sabbah of being overly political and pro-Palestinian. Jerusalem mayor Teddy Kollek, for example, became furious with Sabbah for cancelling the traditional Palm Sunday procession from the Mount of Olives into Jerusalem's Old City in 1989 and 1990 in protest of repressive Israeli military measures in the Occupied Territories. While the Greek Orthodox Church in Palestine and Israel is larger than the Roman Catholic communion, Sabbah was, from the Israeli government's perspective, the most visible church leader, thanks to the Roman Catholic Church's worldwide reach. Because of this high profile, and because of Sabbah's ecumenical efforts to unify church leaders around common causes, the Israeli state also found Sabbah to be the most threatening church leader.

Over the next two decades, Sabbah released a series of pastoral letters and theological reflections in which he sought to answer the challenge of reading the Bible and thinking through claims about election and promises of the land in a way that does not justify the dispossession of one people at the hands of another. In *Reflections on the Presence of the Church in the Holy Land*, the Latin Patriarchate's theological commission, led by Sabbah, underscored the distinctive voice that the church in the Holy Land brings to the church's worldwide reflections on Judaism, Zionism, and the State of Israel. Sabbah and the other members of the theological commission observed that the church in Palestine is "the only Local Church that encounters the Jewish people in a state that is defined as Jewish and where the Jews are the dominant and empowered majority, a reality that dates from 1948. Furthermore, the ongoing conflict between the State of Israel and the Arab world, and in particular between Palestinians and Israelis, means that the national identity of our faithful is locked in conflict with the national identity of the majority of the Jews." The

Palestinian church, Sabbah and his theological commission colleagues contended, must thus be included in the world-wide church's task of reflecting on the mystery of God's relationship with the Jewish people and what that means regarding the State of Israel. Under Sabbah's leadership, the Latin Patriarchate's theological commission underscored that "the official teaching of the Roman Catholic Church regarding the Jews and Judaism is also our teaching." The commission continued: "With the entire Church, we meditate on the roots of our faith in the Old Testament, which we share with the Jewish people, and in the New Testament that is written largely by Jews about Jesus of Nazareth. With the entire Church, we regret the attitudes of contempt, the conflicts and the hostility that have marked the history of Jewish-Christian relations."[11]

Sabbah developed his thinking about covenant, election, land, and the State of Israel most fully in his fourth pastoral letter, *Reading the Bible Today in the Land of the Bible*, issued in 1993. In that letter, Sabbah argued that the challenge for a Palestinian Christian theologian writing about election in general is to do so without justifying claims of superiority over others or of the right to dispossess others. Thus, Sabbah stressed that "God's choice of a person or people should not be a cause of pride in those chosen, nor rejection of those not chosen. It is in the humility lived by both, and in their common vision of God's action, that they will come together in love, justice and finally to reconciliation." Rather than a triumphalist statement about the superiority or privileges due to the elect people, God's election of a people (be it the Jewish people or the church) testifies first to God's freedom and second to the

11. Diocesan Theological Commission of the Latin Patriarchate of Jerusalem, *Reflections on the Presence of the Church in the Holy Land*, 8–10.

responsibilities election entails. Election represents God's free and gratuitous initiative. As such, election does not designate superior status, but rather a responsibility to be exercised before God and one's fellow humans. To use God's election of a people in order to justify land claims that dispossess others is fundamentally to distort the meaning of election, for "God cannot permit His love for one people to become an injustice for another people."[12]

Sabbah recognized that some biblical passages do present dramatic, horrific acts of violence committed by the elect against the non-elect (Canaanites and others) as responses to God's commands and as the fulfillment of covenantal promises (e.g., Deuteronomy 7). Given how these texts depict the ethnic cleansing of a native people and how religious Zionists, both Jewish and Christian, have drawn on the conquest narratives as divine precedent and justification, such texts represent a theological scandal for many Palestinian Christians, making it difficult for some to accept Old Testament narratives about and promises to the people of Israel as Scripture. Displaced Palestinians hearing God tell the Israelites that "I gave you a land on which you had not labored, and towns that you had not built, and you live in them; you eat the fruit of vineyards and oliveyards that you did not plant" (Joshua 24:13) cannot but think of their own demolished homes and villages and confiscated fields and houses.

While acknowledging the difficulty experienced by some Palestinian Christians in receiving the people of Israel's story as their story, Sabbah emphasized that the Palestinian church must not succumb to the Marcionite temptation of jettisoning the Old Testament, stressing that the Old and New Testaments are interconnected and inextricable for Christians. Having been deprived of land,

12. Sabbah, *Reading the Bible*, 48, 54.

Palestinian Christians should not allow themselves to be deprived of the richness of Scripture. The problem, Sabbah maintained, lies in the ideological distortion of Scripture to justify political programs of conquest and dispossession today, not with Scripture itself. If, he argued, "some manipulate the sacred Scriptures, this is not a reason to abandon our faith in our Scriptures. On the contrary, it is not the Word of God but the manipulation that we must denounce and correct."[13]

To counter what he considered ideologically distorted readings of the Bible, Sabbah offered Palestinian Christians several hermeneutical strategies for interpreting the conquest narratives of the Old Testament. First, Sabbah noted the multivocal character of the Old Testament witness: alongside passages commanding violence and conquest, one finds condemnations and corrections of violence. Secondly, Sabbah stressed, Christians should understand biblical revelation as progressive in character, with God's people gradually receiving a clearer picture of God and God's redeeming work. Finally, Scripture must be read as a unity, as a "single book," with any one incident or passage interpreted in the light of the entirety of the scriptural witness. Not only must Scripture be read as a unity, it should be interpreted in the light of the culmination of Scripture's revelation in Jesus Christ. Biblical passages seemingly justifying violence and dispossession thus cannot, Sabbah insisted, be deployed unproblematically to underwrite the same today, but must be understood in the complex context of the multivocal biblical witness, the progressive character of biblical revelation, and the culmination of that revelation in Jesus Christ.[14]

13. Ibid., 35–36.
14. Ibid., 38–39.

Against those who would treat the Bible as a land deed, Sabbah turned to Scripture itself (citing Leviticus 25:23; 1 Chronicles 29:15; and Psalm 39:12) to insist that the land ultimately belongs not to a chosen people, but to God— before God, the inhabitants of the land are as aliens and tenants. Israel in the Bible was not the absolute owner of the land, but was "only God's guest." Life in the land, moreover, was not an unconditional promise, but was contingent on exercising justice and righteousness in the land. As Sabbah observed, "the chosen people were required to remain worthy of the land, by observing God's law. They had to remain faithful to the grace they had received."[15] Any claims about a supposed right to the land today, Sabbah concluded, thus must ask the question of whether the claimants practice justice and righteousness in the land.

Furthermore, in framing his biblical theology of land, Sabbah appealed to the progressive character of revelation that he underscores in his discussion of the Bible. "The concept of the land has then evolved throughout different stages of Revelation," Sabbah contended, "beginning with the physical, geographical, and political concept and ending up with the spiritual and symbolic meaning. The worship of God is no longer linked to a specific land."[16] Christians cannot, therefore, attribute any ultimate theological significance to projects aimed at establishing political control over particular territories, but should instead seek to ensure that the dignity of all individuals and all peoples in any land under any political configuration is respected and secured.

What, however, of the land promises to the people first called Israel? If God's covenant with the Jewish people has not been abolished, just as the law and the prophets are not abolished, but rather fulfilled, in Jesus (Matthew

15. Ibid., 51.
16. Ibid., 52.

5:17), do the land promises remain valid? Sabbah's answer to such questions was two-fold. First, he insisted that one must distinguish "between the religious fact represented by the Jewish people, with its duties, obligations and religious responsibilities, and the political fact of a modern sovereign state which this people can establish": biblical Israel and the modern nation-state of Israel cannot be collapsed one into the other. Second, Sabbah argued that recognizing the Jewish people's attachment to the land need not translate into theological support for the State of Israel or into theological justification for a nation-state form of landedness. "We respect this relationship [with the land] by which the Jewish people identify with the religion revealed to them by God," he observed. "But we do not believe that this religious identification implies in itself a political right."[17] Christians should not attribute theological significance to the creation of the State of Israel. As *Notes on the Correct Way to Present Jews and Judaism in Preaching and Catechesis in the Roman Catholic Church*, the Vatican's follow-up document to *Nostra Aetate*, states: "The existence of the State of Israel and its political options should be envisaged not in a perspective which is in itself religious, but in their reference to the common principles of international law." Christians should seek to understand Jewish religious attachment to the land, "without however making their own any particular religious interpretation of this relationship."[18]

The church should therefore not link the vital task of renewing and revising its teaching on Judaism to a theological legitimatizing of the State of Israel. To the extent that the global church remains silent about the dispossession that

17. Ibid., 54–55.

18. Committee for Religious Relations with the Jews, *Notes on the Correct Way to Present Jews and Judaism in Preaching and Catechesis in the Roman Catholic Church*, VI, 1.

Zionism has meant for Palestinians, it makes Palestinians pay the price for the sins of the Western church's anti-Semitism. However, rather than pressing the global church from exchanging its explicit or implicit embrace of Zionism for pro-Palestinian advocacy, Sabbah instead counters that the church should be neither pro-Israeli nor pro-Palestinian, affirming the dignity of both Israelis and Palestinians as created in God's image, and should seek peace in the land that upholds that dignity and provides landed security for both Palestinians and Israelis. Likewise, affirmation of the dignity of all peoples in turn requires opposition to any political arrangements that exclude or oppress and to any theologies that justify such oppression or exclusion. To the extent that Zionism is bound up with such dispossession and exclusion, Christians following Sabbah's lead will either be non-Zionist or anti-Zionist, while also working for the landed security of Palestinians and Israeli Jews alike.

This chapter has examined different Christian justifications for Zionism. For Christian Zionists, Jewish return to the land and the establishment of a Jewish state represent the partial fulfillment of apocalyptic hope. For other Christians, concerned with atoning for Christian legacies of anti-Semitism and theological anti-Judaism, embrace of Zionism and defense of modern-day Israel flow from a commitment to defending Jewish security in a post-Holocaust world. Palestinian Christians, meanwhile, vigorously contest Christian Zionism as a heretical theology that privileges Israeli Jewish over Palestinian well-being—and in some instances underwrites visions of the ethnic cleansing of Palestinians. Palestinian Christian theologians also object to Palestinians (Christians and Muslims) being asked to pay the price for the Western church's anti-Semitism and to their exclusion from post-Holocaust theological reflection about God's enduring covenant with the Jewish people, Zionism, and the State of Israel. As the global church continues this grappling with its history of theological anti-Judaism and its discernment of how to understand the interplay among election, biblical land promises, and Zionism, the inclusion of Palestinian Christian theologians like Michel Sabbah in those conversations will be essential.

QUESTIONS FOR DISCUSSION

1. Have you encountered Christian Zionism in your church? In popular media?

2. What critiques do Palestinian Christians have of Christian Zionism?

3. Have you witnessed anti-Judaism in church settings, such as in preaching or hymns? Or attempts by preachers or worship leaders to address anti-Judaism? Have you been part of congregations that have made connections with local synagogues or Jewish leaders? What did those connections look like?

4. What are ways that Catholic and Protestant churches have revised traditional teachings about Judaism following the Holocaust?

5. Why are Palestinian Christians wary of theological claims that God's covenant with the Jewish people remains unbroken?

6. What are key themes in Michel Sabbah's biblical theology of land?

4

A SHARED PALESTINIAN-ISRAELI FUTURE?

THE PRECEDING CHAPTERS SURVEYED the history of the Palestinian-Israeli conflict and examined how Christians, particularly Palestinian Christians, have thought theologically about the conflict. Attention in this concluding chapter now shifts to an assessment of what hope can be had for the conflict's transformation. After an overview of the current status of the key issues in the Palestinian-Israeli conflict that peace negotiations have sought (unsuccessfully) to address, focus turns to critiques of the peace process for functioning to deepen Israeli control over the Occupied Territories while simultaneously advancing a politics of partition that leaves Palestinians in the Occupied Territories confined to ever more tightly circumscribed spaces. That examination leads to an overview of the varying reasons why an increasing number of Israelis and Palestinians question the viability or desirability of a two-state solution to the conflict.

This overview of the present-day state of the Israeli-Palestinian conflict and the moribund peace process will give good grounds for pessimism about the possibility of the conflict's transformation. Yet, following the lead of the Palestinian Christian authors of the *Kairos Palestine Document* who describe their efforts as a "cry of hope beyond all hope," this book concludes with a theological assessment of hope's persistence within the bleak realities of Palestine and Israel today, a hope that animates the actions of Palestinians and Israelis struggling for justice and shared life in the land.[1]

STATUS OF KEY ISSUES IN THE CONFLICT

The Oslo II Accords signed in 1994 identified a set of final status issues to be negotiated during a five-year interim period. Subsequent negotiations have failed to reach agreement on these final status issues. Put more bluntly, the peace process has been stagnant for almost twenty years: the future of Palestine and Israel is not being shaped by joint Israeli-Palestinian negotiations, but rather by unilateral Israeli actions that are reconfiguring the land's geography and are, many observers contend, eclipsing the possibility of a viable two-state solution to the Israeli-Palestinian conflict. Yet, however hobbled, the Palestinian-Israeli peace process persists, at least on paper. When negotiations have been revived every few years over the past two decades, Palestinian and Israeli negotiators have returned to the same set of basic issues, issues whose resolution will be essential to any negotiated settlement between Israelis and Palestinians. This section examines each of these issues in turn, outlining

1. Kairos Palestine, *A Moment of Truth*, Introduction.

the respective positions that Palestinian and Israeli negotiators have staked out.

Borders, Security, and Water

A key element of the final status negotiations is the establishment of permanent borders. Palestinian negotiators have held to the position that the future Palestinian state will be established in all of the Occupied Territories, with the 1949 Armistice Line, or Green Line, as the border between the Palestinian and Israeli states. Israeli negotiators have responded by claiming that such borders would be untenable on security grounds, while also insisting on the incorporation of Israeli settlement blocs into Israel as part of any final status agreement. Maintaining its military control over the Jordan Valley and the West Bank border with the Hashemite Kingdom of Jordan is essential for Israel's security, its negotiators maintain, as is the future Palestinian state being demilitarized. Palestinian negotiators, in turn, have responded that while they are open to the demilitarization of the future Palestinian state, they cannot accept for the future sovereign state of Palestine not to have control over its borders.

Post-Oslo negotiations have discussed potential land swaps that would incorporate major settlement blocs into Israel while adding an equal amount of land to the envisioned Palestinian state. Yet these negotiations have foundered. In the meantime, Israel has built a series of walls and militarized fences deep inside the West Bank, creating *de facto* borders that deviate significantly from the Green Line. Israel calls this system of barriers a security fence, while Palestinians refer to it as a segregation barrier or apartheid wall. Coupled with an extensive network of roadblocks, military checkpoints, and Israeli-only roads, this separation barrier works to restrict Palestinians in the Occupied Territories to ever more confined parcels of disconnected territory.

Final status negotiations will also have to resolve the question of control over water resources—both from the Jordan River and from West Bank aquifers. For now, Israel exercises control over the vast majority of these water resources—in many instances, the path of Israel's segregation barrier has furthered isolated Palestinians from West Bank water resources. As a result, Israeli settlements enjoy uninterrupted access to water, while Palestinian communities receive limited running water and must carefully ration water supplies, with many Palestinian households receiving less water than the minimum amount the World Health Organization deems necessary.

Settlements

Since 1967, successive Israeli governments, in contravention of international law, have allowed or actively supported the establishment of civilian settlements for Israelis within the Occupied Territories. Palestinians often refer to these Israeli settlements as colonies. As an occupying power, Israel is bound by the Geneva Convention on the Protection of Civilian Persons in a Time of War. This international treaty, often referred to as the Fourth Geneva Convention, prohibits occupying powers from moving their civilian populations into occupied territories. Accordingly, most international law experts view Israeli settlements in East Jerusalem and the West Bank as illegal, even as the State of Israel claims that the territories are "administered," not "occupied," and so not subject to the Fourth Geneva Convention.

Settlements have expanded in size and number under both Labor- and Likud-led governments, growing three-fold in population since the signing of the Oslo Accords in the first half of the 1990s. This unrelenting expansion of settlements has deepened Israel's matrix of control over the Occupied Territories. Today, an estimated 400,000 Israeli settlers live in the West Bank, while another 400,000 dwell in East Jerusalem. For many settlers, particularly those in settlements close to the Green Line, living in the settlements is primarily an economic choice. Other settlers are motivated by religious nationalist ideologies.

Jerusalem

Since its founding, Israel has declared Jerusalem to be its eternal capital. Following its conquest of East Jerusalem, including the Old City, in 1967, successive Israeli governments have also insisted that Jerusalem as its capital remain unified. Extensive settlements within occupied East Jerusalem, housing hundreds of thousands of Israelis, have solidified Israeli control over the city. The PLO, meanwhile, envisions East Jerusalem, including the Old City, as the capital of the future State of Palestine. While East Jerusalemite Palestinians have residency permits issued by the State of Israel, their status in the city is precarious: the Israeli state severely restricts Palestinian building in the city, and East Jerusalemites risk losing their residency permits if they live outside the city for an extended period of time. East Jerusalem has systematically been cut off from the rest of the West Bank through Israeli settlement construction and networks of checkpoints, roadblocks, and walls. At the same time, some Palestinian neighborhoods of East Jerusalem have ended up on the West Bank side of the segregation wall, with residents of those neighborhoods now in danger of losing their right to residency in Jerusalem.

For Jews, Muslims, and Christians, Jerusalem is a holy city. Jerusalem's Old City is home to the Church of the Holy Sepulcher, site of Jesus's crucifixion, death, and resurrection. The conflict about sovereignty over Jerusalem encompasses conflict over control of the Holy Esplanade, called *al-Haram ash-Sharif* (the Noble Sanctuary) by Muslims and *Har HaBayit* (the Temple Mount) by Jews. In peace negotiations, Israel and the PLO have both insisted on sovereign control over Jerusalem's Old City, including the Haram/ Temple Mount. This esplanade within Jerusalem's Old City is home to the third holiest site within Islam, the al-Aqsa Mosque, built to commemorate the prophet Muhammad's Night Journey from Mecca to Jerusalem. The Haram also contains the Dome of the Rock, a monument built in the late seventh century CE over a rock that Muslims identify as the place from which Muhammad ascended into heaven, accompanied by the angel Jibril (Gabriel).

For Jews, the site is significant as the location of the First and Second Temples. The Second Temple, once the ritual center of Jewish life in the land, was destroyed by the Romans in 70 CE. Within rabbinic Judaism, the restoration of the Temple was part of the eschatological hopes of redemption with the coming of the promised messiah. For centuries, Jewish pilgrims to Jerusalem have gathered at the Western Wall, or *kotel*, part of an expansion of the Second Temple constructed by Herod, to mourn the Temple's destruction, giving the site its colloquial name, the Wailing Wall. (Muslims call the wall *al-buraq*, identifying it by the name of the winged steed that transported the prophet Muhammad from Mecca to Jerusalem.) Traditionally, rabbinic rulings have held that Jews should not enter the Temple Mount, for fear of accidentally walking over the site of the

Temple's Holy of Holies, where the Ark of the Covenant was kept and to which only the High Priest was allowed entrance one day each year. Some rabbis within Israel's religious nationalist stream, however, hold that Jews can enter certain parts of the Temple Mount. Meanwhile, some Jewish groups, like the Temple Mount Faithful, work to create implements to be used upon the messiah's return and the restoration of the Temple (and, presumably, the destruction of the Islamic sites on the Mount).

Since Israel's conquest of East Jerusalem in 1967, Israel has held sovereignty over the Noble Sanctuary/Temple Mount. However, shortly after the conquest, Israeli military leader Moshe Dayan met with Muslim *waqf* (religious property) officials to formulate a new status quo for entry into the Haram. According to the status quo agreed upon, non-Muslims would be allowed into the Haram, but would not be allowed to pray. In recent years, the status quo has frayed significantly as some religious Zionists have increasingly chafed at and challenged the restrictions on prayer and with *waqf* officials defensively restricting access to the Haram by non-Muslims out of fear that the State of Israel was planning to change the status quo.

Refugee Return

Around five million Palestinians are registered as refugees with the United Nations Relief and Works Agency (UNRWA), of which more than one-third live in 58 UNRWA-operated refugee camps across the Middle East. Palestinians, citing United Nations General Assembly Resolution 194, insist that these refugees have a right to return to their homes from which they were displaced in 1948. For Israeli Jews, however, the prospect of Palestinian refugee return appears as an existential threat, as the return of Palestinian refugees in any appreciable number would jeopardize the Jewish demographic majority in Israel. The return of Palestinian refugees to what is now Israel, from this perspective, runs counter to a two-state solution to the Palestinian-Israeli conflict, for it would result not in a Jewish state alongside a Palestinian state, but rather in two Palestinian states.

Some Israeli negotiators have argued that any discussions of compensation for Palestinian refugees must happen together with talks about compensation to Jews pressured to leave surrounding Arab states following the 1948 war. Palestinian negotiators respond that any Jewish claims to lost properties in those Arab countries should be handled as part of Israeli diplomatic engagements with those countries, rather than as part of Israeli-Palestinian bilateral negotiations.

So-called Track Two efforts (diplomatic efforts by non-state actors) to formulate a final status agreement have sought ways to find an approach to the Palestinian refugee question acceptable to both parties. The Nusseibeh-Ayalon (2002) and Geneva Initiative (2003) plans, for example, both involve Israel's acknowledgment of its responsibility for the Palestinian refugee plight, a recognition of the right of return in principle, and compensation to refugees for properties confiscated by Israel, but with limited exercise of the right of return in practice: these plans would thus greatly restrict any actual Palestinian refugee return. Negative reactions to these plans by refugee advocacy groups reflected concerns among Palestinian refugees about the PLO's perceived readiness to relinquish the right of return in exchange for Palestinian statehood.

Recent Israeli governments, meanwhile, have insisted that the PLO not only recognize Israel (which it has already done as part of the Oslo Accords), but also recognize Israel as a Jewish state. The PLO has balked at this demand on the grounds that it has recognized Israel, that it is up to Israel how it defines itself, and that states do not provide diplomatic recognition of how other states define themselves (e.g., the United States does not recognize Saudi Arabia as an Islamic state, but simply as Saudi Arabia). For their part, Palestinian citizens of Israel, who represent 20 percent of Israel's population, object to demands on Palestinians to recognize Israel as a Jewish state, viewing such demands as counter to their push for greater equality within Israel. Israel, meanwhile, has highlighted Palestinian refusal to recognize Israel as a Jewish state as purported evidence of Palestinian intransigence and rejectionism.

Some proponents of Palestinian refugee return talk about return within the context of a decolonization of Israeli identity. From this perspective, so long as Israeli settler-colonial practices and systems that privilege Israeli Jews over Palestinians (be it in the Occupied Territories or within Israel) remain in place, peace will remain elusive. Such decolonization would not necessarily mean a renunciation of Zionism—although it would arguably call for a change in how Zionism is understood. The late Palestinian-American intellectual Edward Said avoided talking about "de-Zionization," affirming the right of Israeli Jews to assert "their connection to the land, so long as it doesn't keep the others [Palestinians] out so manifestly." What is called for instead of disavowing "Zionism" as a word, Said contended, is a "transformation" of the Israeli-Palestinian reality from one of exclusion, discrimination, and dispossession to one of mutuality. Said did not preclude the possibility that Zionist visions might emerge that would simultaneously affirm Jewish connection to the land and advocate for a polity that leaves behind discriminatory practices of dispossession.[2]

2. Said, *Power, Politics, and Culture*, 451–52.

THE ENDS OF THE PEACE PROCESS

To speak of the end, as in death, of the Israeli-Palestinian peace process is probably premature. After all, the Oslo framework that established the Palestinian National Authority in the Gaza Strip and parts of the West Bank remains in place, while both parties proclaim their supposed readiness to return to negotiations. That said, the peace process undeniably appears to be stalled for the foreseeable future: Israel currently faces little pressure to change the status quo in the Occupied Territories. The United States under the Trump administration has abandoned all pretense of being an honest broker in the Palestinian-Israeli conflict, breaking with international consensus and the U.S.'s own long-standing policy to recognize Jerusalem as Israel's capital and ceasing in some State Department publications to refer to occupied territories. Moreover, Palestinian political disarray means that Palestinians would enter any renewed negotiations in a significantly weakened position. The end of the peace process may not have arrived in the sense of the peace process definitively collapsing, yet no forward momentum has been made for a long time, nor is any progress on the horizon.

One can, however, also speak about the ends of the peace process in terms of outcomes. While the peace process has not produced a permanent peace agreement between the State of Israel and an independent State of Palestine, one can nevertheless rightly observe other outcomes. One significant outcome has been Palestinian political fragmentation. While the geographical fragmentation of the Occupied Territories over the past quarter century is undoubtedly not the sole cause of Palestinian political disarray, the geographical splintering of the Occupied Territories has certainly contributed to the political fracturing of the Palestinian body politic. The mass demonstrations along Gaza's border with Israel organized in the spring of 2018 under the slogan of the Great March of Return, many analysts have suggested, represent an attempt by Palestinian activists to forge a new political unity, bypassing and marginalizing traditional political parties (even as those parties have sought to gain legitimacy by associating themselves with the march). How durable such efforts at unity will be in the face of the forces of fragmentation remains to be seen.

The peace process initiated in the early 1990s has also proceeded hand-in-hand with, and has arguably served as a cover for, Israel's ongoing unilateral separation from Palestinians inside the Occupied Territories, The peace process, its critics contend, has functioned as an Israeli exercise in managing and solidifying, rather than ending, the occupation. This process of what Israeli military theorists and politicians have referred to as *hafrada*, or separation, does not entail Israeli withdrawal from or relinquishing of control over the Occupied Territories. Rather, *hafrada* involves the strengthening of what Israeli sociologist Jeff Halper termed the *matrix of control*, a system made up of the separation walls and electronically monitored fences, checkpoints, roadblocks, Israeli-only roads, and more. This matrix of control restricts Palestinians in the Occupied Territories to ever smaller parcels of land. The matrix of control also occupies Palestinian time, rendering Palestinian daily life subject to the unpredictable whims of military authority.

The ongoing construction and expansion of Israeli settlements in the Occupied Territories strengthens this matrix of control, as the infrastructure of Israel's military occupation extends to connect the settlements in the Occupied Territories to Israel within the pre-1967 border of the Armistice Line. The Israeli doctrine of *hafrada* has thus worked not only to separate Israelis from Palestinians in the

Occupied Territories and Palestinians in the Occupied Territories from one another, but also to progressively erase the Green Line for Israelis who can travel unobstructed from Israel into the settlements, while Palestinian movement is tightly controlled, monitored, delayed, and impeded.

Even if one stipulates that the neighbor in Robert Frost's poem, "Mending Wall," is correct that "good fences make good neighbors" (something that Frost's poem itself does not clearly endorse), Israel's separation walls and barriers have not functioned as good fences. Rather than being constructed along the 1949 Armistice line that Palestinians insist must serve as the border in a permanent peace agreement between independent and sovereign Israeli and Palestinian states, these dividing walls and militarized fences have cut deep into the Occupied Territories, creating *de facto*, if not *de jure*, new borders. Through these electronically monitored fences and walls, Israel has not established and nurtured neighborly relations with Palestinians, but has instead operated as a *carceral state*, imprisoning and confining Palestinians within circumscribed territory and severely limiting—or even completely prohibiting—movement out of it. The confinement of the two million Palestinians within what multiple human rights organizations have called the open-air prison of the Gaza Strip displays Israel's carceral regime at the macro-level. In the village of Beit Ijza in the West Bank, meanwhile, Israel's carceral regime operates at the micro-level, with walls and fences completely surrounding the home of the Sabri family, with the family forced to rely on the Israeli military (whom they contact through an intercom installed at the locked gate to the cage that surrounds them) when they want to come or go. Throughout the Occupied Territories, the Israeli policy of *hafrada* has functioned to limit, confine, control, and even imprison Palestinians.

While the dividing walls and fences and other mecha-
nisms of control constructed as part of this unilateral separation process have been presented by Israel to the world
as a set of security measures aimed at preventing Palestinian attacks on Israeli targets, the *hafrada* doctrine also
responds to what Israeli politicians from the center-left
to the right have referred to as the "demographic threat"
posed by Palestinians. Arnon Soffer, professor of geography at the University of Haifa, has led the charge in loudly
warning of the danger posed to Israel of the higher overall
Palestinian birthrate when compared to Israeli Jews as a
group. Given these higher birthrates, Soffer argues, Israeli
Jews will soon be a minority within the land encompassed
by Israel and the Occupied Territories. Moreover, some
demographers predict that over the coming decades, the
percentage of Palestinian Arabs among Israeli citizens
(that is, excluding Palestinians in the Occupied Territories)
will steadily increase from its current level of 20 percent.
Current Israeli Prime Minister Binyamin Netanyahu has
expressed concern about this trend, while other Israeli Jewish observers have described Palestinian citizens of Israel
as a potential "fifth column." Some Israeli politicians have
even argued that parts of Israel with dense Palestinian Arab
populations should be relinquished to a future Palestinian
state in exchange for Israeli annexation of its settlement
blocs in the Occupied Territories. For Palestinians within
Israel, the passage by the Israeli parliament, the Knesset, of
the so-called "nation-state" law in July 2018 represented a
declaration of their status as second-class citizens, a stark
pronouncement in foundational Israeli law of the numer-
ous ways Palestinian citizens of Israel face discrimination
by the state on a daily basis.

While the discourse of fear over the demographic
threat posed by Palestinians has been roundly condemned

by Israeli human rights organizations and other observers, Israeli political discourse from the center-left to the right has played on these fears for the past two decades. Former Israeli Prime Minister Ehud Olmert of the right-wing Likud party described his government's policy towards the Occupied Territories and negotiations with the Palestinians as seeking to secure maximum land within a minimal number of Palestinians. Former Israeli Prime Minister Ehud Barak of the center-left Labor party deployed an election campaign slogan of "Us here, them there," warning that without unilateral separation from the Palestinians in the Occupied Territories, Israel would find it increasingly challenging to rebut charges that it oversees an apartheid-style regime in the Occupied Territories. The demographic panic fostered by this political discourse has in turn been deployed to justify Israel's *hafrada* policy. While the peace process arguably hit a dead end under Olmert, Barak, and other Israeli Prime Ministers during the past two decades, the end, or goal, of establishing greater separation from—as well as greater control over—Palestinians in the Occupied Territories has been achieved.

TWO STATES, ONE STATE, OR?

In the face of the Israeli matrix of control extended across the Occupied Territories and the ongoing expansion of Israeli settlements in the West Bank, many outside analysts, along with an increasing number of Palestinians and Israelis, question whether a two-state solution to the Palestinian-Israeli conflict remains viable or desirable. Some politicians and activists on the Israeli right press to hasten the death of the two-state solution and push for Israeli annexation of the Occupied Territories. Israeli critics of these calls for annexation observe that if annexation granted citizenship to

Palestinians in the Occupied Territories, then Israel's Jewish demographic majority would be erased, but if Israel did not grant such citizenship, then comparisons of Israel's rule to apartheid-era South Africa would be hard to rebut.

On the Palestinian side, meanwhile, the Palestinian National Authority and the PLO maintain a commitment to the two-state solution, even as Palestinians wonder if the geographic basis for such a solution has been erased by the Israeli matrix of control. The Islamist Hamas movement, for its part, while officially adhering to its stated goal of liberating all of Palestine as *waqf* (religious property), has indicated a readiness to consider a long-term truce, or *hudna*, with Israel based on Palestinian statehood established along the Green Line.

To be sure, the obituary for the two-state solution has been written multiple times over the past quarter century. Starting in the mid-1990s, a steady stream of Palestinian officials, Jordanian government leaders, Israeli peace activists, and others have warned that the window on a two-state solution would soon close—and yet the two-state solution has continued to set the terms for the peace process and for international diplomatic deliberations about the conflict.

The endurance of the two-state solution can be explained in part by how Israeli governments have redefined what such a solution would entail. Israel's center-right Likud party resisted talk of Palestinian statehood for many years after the Oslo process got underway. Then, in 2003, Israeli Prime Minister Ariel Sharon of the Likud party endorsed a two-state solution; his Likud successor as Prime Minister, Binyamin Netanyahu, has done likewise. Yet this Israeli acceptance of a two-state solution has not been an embrace of the two-state solution as Palestinians understand it—namely, as the creation of a Palestinian state in all of the West Bank, East Jerusalem, and the Gaza Strip (with possible one-to-one land swaps). Rather, the Israeli government's rhetorical embrace of a two-state solution reflects its policy of *hafrada*: if Palestinians are willing to accept statehood within the circumscribed bounds created by the walls, fences, and matrix of control that Israel has established, then Israel would also agree to Palestinian statehood on those terms.

Not surprisingly, such a vision of the two-state solution is a non-starter for Palestinians. Some Palestinians and Israelis have begun to argue that as prospects for a two-state solution based on the Green Line and on the United Nations "land-for-peace" resolutions 242 and 338 dim to the point of extinguishing, alternatives to the two-state solution must be explored. Some argue that Palestinians should press for one state in all of Palestine and Israel in which all would enjoy equal citizenship. Proponents of the one-state approach argue that there already is a one-state reality in Palestine and Israel—a discriminatory reality in which the sovereign Israeli state rules over millions of stateless Palestinians. One-state advocates hope for a day in which this discriminatory one-state reality might be transformed into a one-state reality of equality.

Other Palestinians and Israelis press for a binational federation between Israel and Palestine that would recognize communal identities within a common political framework, while still others advocate for the eventual formation of a regional confederation including Israel, Palestine, and Jordan. Still others envision Palestine and Israel as two completely overlapping, parallel states in which people would carry their national identities and citizenship with them while allowing for free movement in the land for all.

These creative exercises in imagining alternatives to the grim, present-day reality of an entrenched military occupation offer tentative hope of other possible futures.

Defenders of the two-state solution, however, respond that if a two-state solution is deemed unrealistic, then these speculative visions must be deemed still more unrealistic. For those concerned with justice, peace, and mutuality for Palestinians and Israelis, the status quo of military occupation and Palestinian confinement within a matrix of control are clearly unacceptable. Yet hope for realizing alternatives to the status quo—in the form of a two-state solution, the establishment of one state of all its citizens, or something else—is elusive and fragile.

A THEOLOGY OF *SUMUD* AND HOPE

The Kairos Palestine authors were soberly realistic regarding the bleak state of the Palestinian-Israeli conflict. "We see nothing in the present or future except ruin and destruction," they wrote in 2009, pointing to growing trends both within Israel and Occupied Territories towards exclusivist divisions and partitions and to a Palestinian resistance in disarray. Yet, they continued, "Hope is the capacity to see God in the midst of trouble, and to be co-workers with the Holy Spirit who is dwelling in us. From this vision derives the strength to be steadfast, remain firm and work to change the reality in which we find ourselves."[3] This steadfast hope within a seemingly hopeless reality, or what Palestinians call *sumud*, marks Palestinian Christians theologies.

Palestinian Christian theologies of *sumud* are grounded in the peace of Christ, in the hope that through Jesus Christ God has broken dividing walls of hostility (Ephesians 2:10–20). In the face of a politics of partition animated by nationalist visions, a politics that excludes and uproots, Palestinian Christian theologians testify to the possibility of a future polity and geography not defined by

3. Kairos Palestine, *A Moment of Truth*, 3.2.

walls, fences, checkpoints, and roadblocks, but rather by mutuality and reconciliation. What shape that polity might take is unclear—two states living side-by-side in mutually beneficial interdependence? One state in which all people in the land enjoy equal citizenship? Some other configuration? Yet amidst that uncertainty, Palestinian Christian theologies testify that the politics of violent partition are not the final word.

Palestinian Christian theologies of *sumud*, as shown above, are also characterized by an assertion of Palestinian rootedness in and belonging to the land. Yet this insistence on rootedness and belonging is not an exclusivist claim to the land. Rather, the claim to belong to the land flows from the prior recognition that the land ultimately belongs to God and that before God the people are as aliens and tenants (Leviticus 25:23). For Palestinians and Israelis to inhabit the land rightly, then, entails recognizing one another as fellow aliens and tenants in the land promised by God. Palestinian Christian theologies of *sumud* exist within this tension between a rooted belonging to the land and the unsettling of this belonging. Within this tension, the land no longer appears as the exclusive patrimony of one people, but is revealed as God's possession. This recognition of the land as God's in turn opens new modes of inhabiting the land, a belonging that recognizes others in the land as fellow tenants and aliens before God.

Palestinian Christian theologies of *sumud* express these new ways of inhabiting the land in practical action. One sees this theology of *sumud* in the decades-long efforts of the Palestinian Christians from Iqrit described in this book's introduction to return to the site of their destroyed village. This practical theology of *sumud* insists on Palestinian presence and rootedness in the land, while also, through solidarity with Israeli Jewish activists from organizations like Zochrot, embodying the promise of the land as a space for all.

A theology of *sumud* also animates the Tent of Nations organic farm on land southwest of Bethlehem owned by the Palestinian Christian Nassar family. Using Ottoman-era land laws, the Israeli military government in the Occupied Territories has sought to confiscate this farmland, claiming it as state land, a process it has used across the West Bank to facilitate settlement construction and to establish its matrix of control. The Nassar family has waged an ongoing legal battle against these confiscation orders. At the same time, it created the Tent of Nations as a place for intercultural bridge-building. The Tent of Nations thus expresses through concrete actions a theology of *sumud* that simultaneously asserts belonging and presence while also embracing a vision of the land as a blessing for the nations.

The Sumud Freedom Camp, established in 2017 by a Palestinian Christian organization, Holy Land Trust, together with the Center for Jewish Nonviolence, Combatants for Peace, and others, embodies this witness to an alternative way of inhabiting the land. Together, the participants (including Israeli Jews, Palestinian Christians, Palestinian Muslims, and people from diaspora Jewish communities) established and maintained a camp to provide a nonviolent presence to protect members of the West Bank Palestinian Bedouin community of Sarura who had been evicted from their cave homes by the Israeli military and were seeking to return. While return has not been secured for the people of Sarura, the Sumud Freedom Camp has stood as a sign of hope that a different way of inhabiting the land not shaped by partition and dispossession is possible.

Finally, a theology of *sumud* is a theology of worship. Across Palestine and Israel, Palestinian Christians gather each Sunday for worship, praying and giving praise to God through liturgies whose roots trace back centuries. In many Palestinian churches, congregants also join in singing a more recent Arabic-language hymn with the refrain, "O God of peace, rain peace upon us; O God of peace, fill our hearts with peace; O God of peace, fill our land with peace." As much as (and perhaps more than) any book, pastoral letter, or declaration, the Palestinian church's worship and prayer express its theology of what inhabiting the land should look like. The hymn embodies an expectant plea to God to rain down peace on a parched land where justice and the things that make for peace are sorely wanting. In its petition to God to fill the hearts of God's people with peace, it testifies that the ministry of peacemaking and reconciliation flows from the peace and reconciliation received from God. And finally, the hymn captures a vision of peace pouring forth on the entire land, on all of its peoples—not a counterfeit peace established through exclusion, dispossession, and violence, but rather a peace based on justice that restores and transforms relationships.

The future promised by God through the prophet Micah of a day in which God's children will inhabit the land in peace, justice, and security seems remote in Palestine and Israel today, even illusory. Hopelessness and despair too often seem inescapable. Yet within this despair, hope can be found in the Palestinian church's *sumud*, its steadfast witness not only to its presence but also to a future of shared belonging in the land. Hope for new ways of inhabiting the land can be found in the actions of Palestinian and Israeli peacebuilders in the ruins of Iqrit, the farmland of the Tent of Nations, and the caves of Sarura. May God multiply these signs of hope and, by so doing, fill the land of Palestine and Israel with peace.

QUESTIONS FOR DISCUSSION

1. What are the final status issues at the core of Israeli-Palestinian peace negotiations?

2. Why are Israeli settlements in the Occupied Territories considered illegal under international law?

3. Why is Jerusalem significant for Christians, Muslims, and Jews? List several reasons.

4. How have some Track Two diplomatic initiatives sought to resolve the Palestinian refugee question?

5. What is the Israeli policy of *hafrada*? What factors motivate it?

6. Why do some Palestinians argue that a two-state solution is no longer viable? Offer more than one reason. What are alternatives to a two-state solution?

7. What lessons might Palestinian Christian theologies of *sumud* have for people in other contexts facing dispossession and grappling with the question of how to inhabit the land rightly?

Appendix 1

TIMELINE

1516–1918   Palestine is a part of southern Greater Syria under Ottoman rule; Ottoman Empire controls most of the Middle East.

1880s   Rise of Arab nationalism pressing for independence from the Ottoman Empire based out of present-day Turkey.

1881–1903   First *aliyah* (literally "ascent"), or initial wave of Jewish immigration to historical Palestine, then controlled by the Ottoman Empire; followed wave of attacks on Jewish communities in Russia. Most immigrants (*olim*, or "the ones who ascend") came from Eastern Europe.

1896   Publication of Theodor Herzl's *Der Judenstaat* (The Jewish State).

August 29–31, 1897	First Zionist Congress held in Basel, Switzerland: heralded the establishment of Zionism as an institutional movement. Helmed by Theodor Herzl. Adoption of the "Basel Program" to promote Jewish settlement in Palestine.
1904–1914	Second *aliyah* of Jewish immigrants to historical Palestine (still controlled by the Ottoman Empire), with most immigrants coming from the Russian Empire.
1915–1916	Sykes-Picot secret agreement between France and the United Kingdom about how to divide spheres of influence in anticipation of the successful defeat of the Ottoman Empire during World War I.
November 1917	Balfour Declaration—Declaration of support by Great Britain for "the establishment in Palestine of a national home for the Jewish people," so long as it not "prejudice the civil and religious rights of existing non-Jewish communities in Palestine, or the rights and political status enjoyed by Jews in any other country."
1919–1923	Third *aliyah* of Zionist migration to historical Palestine, after the collapse of the Ottoman Empire and following the Bolshevik Revolution in Russia. US-sponsored King-Crane Commission reports of Arab desires for independence; newly created League of Nations ignores King-Crane and divides Arab lands into entities called mandates, intended to create nation-states.

September 1923	League of Nations gives the United Kingdom a mandate over Palestine (alongside other mandates to the United Kingdom and France over other Arab lands from the Ottoman Empire defeated during World War I).
1929	Intercommunal violence, including the destruction of the centuries-old Jewish community in Hebron, sparked by changes to the status quo at the Western Wall.
1936–1939	Arab Revolt against the British Mandatory Power.
1937	Peel Commission proposal for dividing Mandate Palestine into an Arab state linked to Transjordan, a Jewish state, and a mandatory zone.
1939	British government White Paper laying out a vision for the future of the territory of Mandate Palestine.
1940s	World War II; Holocaust: Nazi regime responsible for death of approximately six million Jews (the *Shoah*); Lebanon becomes independent in 1943; Syria in 1944; Jordan in 1946.
1945	United Nations (UN) established; World War II ends, leaving 100,000 Eastern and Central European Jews in displaced persons camps.

November 1947 — Passage of United Nations General Assembly Resolution 181, also known as the Partition Plan, calling for the division of Mandate Palestine into independent Arab and Jewish states, with international control over the greater Jerusalem area as a *corpus separatum*.

May 14, 1948 — End of the British Mandate for Palestine; Israeli Declaration of Independence.

1948–1949 — Arab-Israeli War of 1948 (known as the War of Independence by Israelis and as the *nakba*, or catastrophe, by Palestinians). Over 400 Palestinian towns and villages were destroyed in the course of the war and its aftermath, with nearly two-thirds of the Palestinian population at the time becoming refugees (over 700,000 persons).

1949 — United Nations General Assembly passes Resolution 194, calling on Israel to allow Palestinian refugees willing to live in peace to return home at the earliest practicable date.

December 8, 1949 — United Nations Relief and Works Agency for Palestine Refugees in the Near East (UNRWA) founded, tasked with meeting the humanitarian needs of Palestinian refugees.

1950   Israel passes the Law of Return, guaranteeing the right of every Jew in the world to settle in Israel, and the Absentee Property Law, leading to extensive confiscation of Palestinian property.

1956   Suez Crisis: Israel, with support from Great Britain and France, attacks Egypt in the Sinai Peninsula with the goals of seizing control of the Suez Canal and of removing Egyptian leader Gamal Abdel Nasser from power.

May 28, 1964   Founding of the Palestine Liberation Organization (PLO).

June 5–10, 1967   Arab-Israeli War between Israel and the surrounding Arab states (often referred to as the Six-Day War by Israelis and as the *naksa*, or setback, by Palestinians), leaving over 400,000 Palestinians displaced. Over the course the war, Israel conquered East Jerusalem and the West Bank from Jordan, the Golan Heights from Syria, and the Gaza Strip and the Sinai Peninsula from Egypt. (Following the 1948 War, Jordan had claimed sovereignty over the West Bank, including East Jerusalem, while Egypt had administered the Gaza Strip.)

June 27–28, 1967   Israel expands the Jerusalem municipality's boundaries to include East Jerusalem and surrounding areas.

November 22, 1967	United Nations Security Council Resolution 242 adopted, calling for peace in exchange for "withdrawal of Israeli armed forces from territories occupied in the recent conflict."
1968–1969	Israeli settlement construction in the Occupied West Bank and Gaza Strip begins. PLO adopts as its goal the creation of a single democratic state in all of Mandate Palestine. Yassir Arafat becomes head of the PLO.
1970	PLO expelled from Jordan in the wake of Black September.
October 6–25, 1973	1973 Arab-Israeli War (also known as the October War or the Yom Kippur War) fought between Israel and an Arab coalition led by Egypt and Syria.
October 22, 1973	Adoption of United Nations Security Council Resolution 338, reaffirming UNSC 242 and its land-for-peace formulation.
October 28, 1974	Arab League recognizes the PLO as the "sole legitimate representative" of the Palestinian people.
September 17, 1978	Camp David Accords signed between Israel and Egypt. This led to the signing on March 26, 1979, of the Egyptian-Israeli Peace Treaty. In 1982, Israel returned the Sinai Peninsula to Egypt.
1980	Israel passes the "Jerusalem Law" declaring a "complete and united" Jerusalem as the capital of Israel.

June 6, 1982   Israeli invasion of Lebanon and attack
               on the PLO headquartered in Lebanon
               begins.

September   Massacre of Palestinians in Sabra and
16–18, 1982   Shatilla refugee camps in Lebanon.

December   Start of the first *intifada* ("shaking off" or
1987   "uprising").

December   Establishment of Hamas (acronym in Ar-
1987   abic for Islamic Resistance Movement),
               an offshoot of the Gaza branch of the
               Egyptian-based Muslim Brotherhood.

November   Palestinian Declaration of Independence,
15, 1988   along with the PLO's statement of
               readiness to engage in multilateral peace
               negotiations involving Israel on the basis
               of UNSC Resolutions 242 and 338 and
               their "land-for-peace" principle.

July 1988   Jordan relinquishes claims on the West
               Bank.

October 30–   Madrid Conference: Multi-lateral peace
November   conference held in Spain that led to bi-
1, 1991   lateral negotiations between Israel and a
               joint Jordanian-Palestinian delegation.

September 13, 1993 Declaration of Principles on Interim Self-Governance Arrangements (also known as the Oslo I Accord) between Israel and the PLO; presented as an initial step towards the implementation of UNSC Resolutions 242 and 338 (the "withdrawal from occupied territories for peace" resolutions). Led to the establishment of the Palestinian National Authority (PNA) in the Gaza Strip and Jericho. Included the PLO's recognition of Israel and Israel's recognition of the PLO as a representative of the Palestinian people.

February 25, 1994 Massacre of 29 and wounding of over 120 Palestinian Muslims during prayer in the Ibrahimi Mosque in Hebron by Baruch Goldstein, a settler from the nearby Israeli settlement of Kiryat Arba.

September 28, 1995 Signing of the Interim Agreement on the West Bank and the Gaza Strip (also known as the Oslo II Accord) by Israel and the PLO. Led to the division of the West Bank into Areas A (supposed Palestinian autonomy over civil and security affairs), B (Palestinian control over civil affairs), and C (full Israeli control).

January 17, 1997 Signing of the Hebron Protocol, which divided the West Bank city of Hebron into Israeli- and Palestinian-controlled areas.

July 2000   Camp David summit convened by the United States in effort to secure final status agreement between Israel and the PLO.

Fall 2000   Start of the second *intifada*, also known as the Al-Aqsa *intifada*, which continues until ca. 2005.

January 2001   Summit in Taba, Egypt, for direct talks between Israel and PLO on a final status agreement.

March–May 2002   Israeli reinvasion and bombardment of Palestinian cities throughout the West Bank (called "Operation Defensive Shield" by Israel).

2002   Nusseibeh-Ayalon Plan: draft Permanent Status Agreement written by Sari Nusseibeh (Palestinian academic and former PLO representative in Jerusalem) and Ami Ayalon (former Israeli intelligence chief).

2002   Arab Peace Initiative advanced by the Arab League.

2002   Israel begins construction of the separation barrier or wall within the Occupied West Bank.

2003   Geneva Accord (or Geneva Initiative): draft Permanent Status Agreement written by former Israeli and Palestinian politicians Yossi Beilin and Yasser Abed Rabbo.

February 2005	Summit in Sharm el-Sheikh, Egypt, in which Israeli and Palestinian leaders agreed to a Road Map for resolving the final status issues developed by the Quartet of the United States, Russia, the European Union, and Great Britain.
2005	Israeli "disengagement" from the Gaza Strip, involving the dismantling of settlements and the withdrawal of troops to the Gaza Strip's borders with Israel. With Israel maintaining full control over what comes into and goes out of the Gaza Strip, international law experts agree that Gaza remains occupied territory.
2006	Hamas wins the Palestinian Legislative Council elections, leading to increased tensions between Hamas and Fatah. In 2007, Hamas takes over control of the Gaza Strip.
December 2008– January 2009	Israeli bombardment of the Gaza Strip and Islamist rocket fire into southern Israel (what Israel called "Operation Cast Lead").
2012	United Nations General Assembly gives non-Member Observer State status to Palestine.
August 2014	Israeli bombardment and temporary reinvasion of the Gaza Strip (what Israel called "Operation Protective Edge").
March 30, 2018	Start of the Great March of Return protests along the Gaza-Israel border.

May 14, 2018	The United States moves its embassy to Jerusalem.
July 19, 2018	Israeli parliament (the Knesset) passes the Basic Law: Israel as the Nation-State of the Jewish People.

Appendix 2

MAPS

Map 1: United Nations General Assembly Resolution 181: Partition Map, 1947

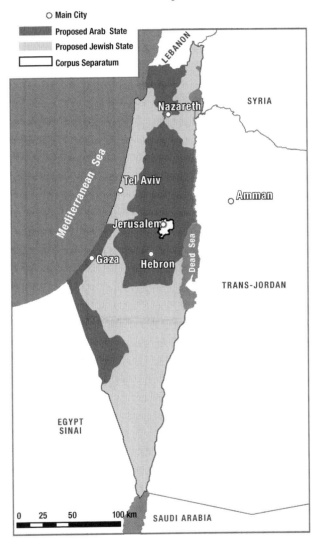

○ Main City

Proposed Arab State

Proposed Jewish State

Corpus Separatum

LEBANON

SYRIA

Nazareth

Mediterranean Sea

Tel Aviv

Amman

Jerusalem

Dead Sea

Gaza

Hebron

TRANS-JORDAN

EGYPT
SINAI

0   25   50   100 km

SAUDI ARABIA

Map 2: The Armistice Line, 1949

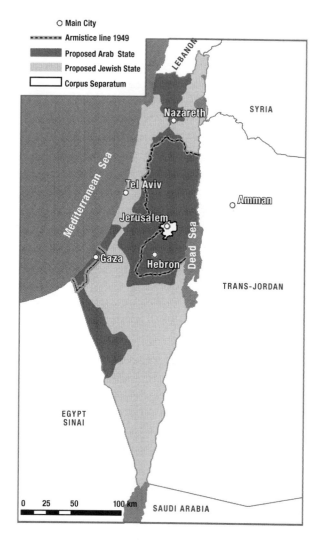

○ Main City
▪▪▪▪▪ Armistice line 1949
■ Proposed Arab State
░ Proposed Jewish State
□ Corpus Separatum

LEBANON

SYRIA

Nazareth

Mediterranean Sea

Tel Aviv

Amman

Jerusalem

Gaza

Hebron

Dead Sea

TRANS-JORDAN

EGYPT
SINAI

0   25   50   100 km

SAUDI ARABIA

Map 3: The Near East after June 1967 War

○ Main City

▪▪▪▪▪▪ Armistice Line 1949

▓▓▓ The Occupied Territories after 1967

███ Demilitarized Zone

Map 4: Oslo II Division of the West Bank

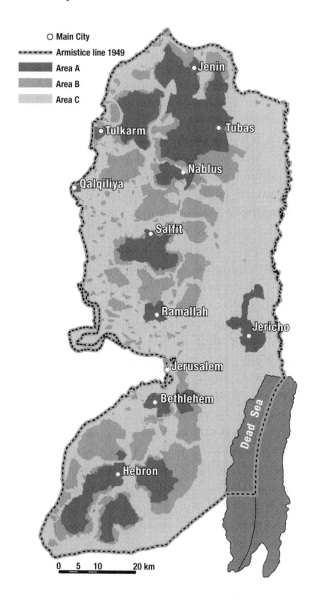

○ Main City
▪▪▪ Armistice line 1949
█ Area A
█ Area B
█ Area C

Jenin

Tulkarm   Tubas

Nablus

Qalqiliya

Salfit

Ramallah   Jericho

Jerusalem

Bethlehem

Dead Sea

Hebron

0   5   10   20 km

Map 5: Segregation Barrier in the West Bank

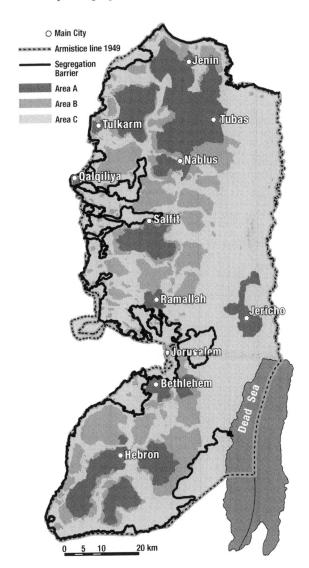

○ Main City
✕✕✕✕ Armistice line 1949
━━━ Segregation Barrier
■ Area A
■ Area B
■ Area C

Jenin

Tulkarm   Tubas

Nablus

Qalqiliya

Salfit

Ramallah   Jericho

Jerusalem

Bethlehem

Dead Sea

Hebron

0 5 10   20 km

WORKS CITED AND
FURTHER READING

CHAPTER ONE

Histories of Zionism and the State of Israel

Buber, Martin. *A Land of Two Peoples: Martin Buber on Jews and Arabs*. Edited by Paul Mendes-Flohr. Chicago: University of Chicago Press, 2005.

Cohen, Hillel. *Year Zero of the Arab-Israeli Conflict: 1929*. Waltham, MA: Brandeis University Press, 2015.

Gorenberg, Gershon. *The Accidental Empire: Israel and the Birth of the Settlements, 1967–1977*. New York: Holt, 2007.

Halper, Jeff. *An Israeli in Palestine: Resisting Dispossession, Redeeming Israel*. London: Pluto, 2008.

Hertzberg, Arthur. *The Zionist Idea: A Historical Analysis and Reader*. New York: Jewish Publication Society, 1997.

Herzl, Theodor. *The Jewish State*. Mineola, NY: Dover, 1989.

Kaplan, Eran, and Derek J. Penslar, eds. *The Origins of Israel, 1882–1948: A Documentary History*. Madison: University of Wisconsin Press, 2011.

Kornberg, Jacques. *Theodor Herzl: From Assimilation to Zionism*. Bloomington, IN: University of Indiana Press, 1993.

Pappé, Ilan. *A History of Modern Palestine: One Land, Two Peoples*. Cambridge: Cambridge University Press, 2006.

Piterberg, Gabriel. *The Returns of Zionism: Myth, Politics, and Scholarship in Israel*. London: Verso, 2008.

Raz-Krakotzkin, Amnon. *Exil et Souveraineté: Judaïsme, Sionisme, et Pensée Binationale*. Paris: La Fabrique, 2007.

Segev, Tom. *One Palestine, Complete: Jews and Arabs under the British Mandate*. London: Picador, 2000.

Shimoni, Gideon. *The Zionist Ideology*. Brandeis University Press, 1995.

Shlaim, Avi. *The Iron Wall: Israel and the Arab World*. New York: Norton, 2001; updated and expanded, 2014.

Modern Palestinian History

Anderson, Benedict. *Imagined Communities: Reflections on the Origin and Spread of Nationalism*. London: Verso, 1991.

Hroub, Khalid. *Hamas: Political Thought and Practice*. Washington, DC: Institute for Palestine Studies, 2000.

Khalidi, Rashid. *Palestinian Identity: The Construction of Modern National Consciousness*. New York: Columbia University Press, 1997.

Kimmerling, Baruch, and Joel Migdal. *The Palestinians: The Making of a People*. Cambridge: Harvard University Press, 1992.

Lybarger, Loren. *Identity and Religion in Palestine: The Struggle between Islamism and Secularism in the Occupied Territories*. Princeton: Princeton University Press, 2007.

Mishal, Shaul, and Avraham Sela. *The Palestinian Hamas: Vision, Violence, and Coexistence*. New York: Columbia University Press, 2006.

Muslih, Muhammad Y. *The Origins of Palestinian Nationalism*. New York: Columbia University Press, 1988.

Pappé, Ilan. *The Ethnic Cleansing of Palestine*. London: Oneworld, 2007.

Pearlman, Wendy. *Violence, Nonviolence, and the Palestinian National Movement*. Cambridge: Cambridge University Press, 2011.

Qumsiyeh, Mazin. *Popular Resistance in Palestine: A History of Hope and Empowerment*. London: Pluto, 2011.

Said, Edward W. *The Question of Palestine*. Reissued edition. New York: Vintage, 1992.

Sayigh, Yezid. *Armed Struggle and the Search for State: The Palestinian National Movement, 1949–1993*. Oxford: Oxford University Press, 2000.

Websites

"Resolution 194." United Nations Relief and Works Administration (UNRWA) website. https://www.unrwa.org/content/resolution-194.

United Nations General Assembly Resolutions: http://www.un.org/en/sections/documents/general-assembly-resolutions/. Includes full text of UNGA 181 (Partition Plan) and UNGA 194 (right of Palestinian refugee return).

Zochrot: https://zochrot.org

CHAPTER TWO

Palestinian Christian Theologies

Al-Liqa' Center. *Theology and the Local Church in the Holy Land.* [Arabic] Bethlehem: Al-Liqa Center, 1988.

Ateek, Naim. *Justice and Only Justice: A Palestinian Theology of Liberation.* Maryknoll, NY: Orbis, 1989.

———. *A Palestinian Christian Cry for Reconciliation.* Maryknoll, NY: Orbis, 2008.

———. *A Palestinian Theology of Liberation: The Bible, Justice, and the Palestine-Israel Conflict.* Maryknoll, NY: Orbis, 2017.

Chacour, Elias. *Blood Brothers.* Grand Rapids: Chosen, 2003

———. *We Belong to the Land: The Story of a Palestinian Israeli who Lives for Peace and Reconciliation.* With Mary E. Jensen. Notre Dame: University of Notre Dame Press, 2001.

Gräbe, Uwe. *Kontextuelle Palästinensische Theologie: Streitbare und Umstrittene Beiträge zum Ökumenischen und Interreligiösen Gespräch.* Erlangen, DE: Erlangen Verlag für Mission und Ökumene, 1999.

Isaac, Munther. *From Land to Lands, from Eden to the Renewed Earth: A Christ-Centered Biblical Theology of the Promised Land.* Carlisle, UK: Langham Monographs, 2015.

Kairos Palestine. *A Moment of Truth: A Word of Faith, Hope, and Love from the Heart of Palestinian Suffering.* Jerusalem: Kairos Palestine, 2009. Available at www.kairospalestine.ps.

Katanacho, Yohanna. *The Land of Christ: A Palestinian Cry.* Eugene, OR: Pickwick, 2013.

Lybarger, Loren. "For Church or Nation? Islamism, Secular-Nationalism, and the Transformation of Christian Identities in Palestine." *Journal of the American Academy of Religion* 75/4 (December 2007) 777–813.

May, Melanie. *Jerusalem Testament: Palestinian Christians Speak, 1988–2008.* Grand Rapids: Eerdmans, 2010.

Raheb, Mitri. *Faith in the Face of Empire: The Bible through Palestinian Eyes.* Maryknoll, NY: Orbis, 2014.

———. *I Am a Palestinian Christian.* Minneapolis: Augsburg Fortress, 1995.

Rantisi, Audeh. *Blessed Are the Peacemakers: The Story of a Palestinian Christian.* Grand Rapids: Zondervan, 1990.

Sabbah, Michel. *Faithful Witness: On Reconciliation and Peace in the Holy Land.* Hyde Park, NY: New City, 2009.

Sabeel Ecumenical Liberation Theology Center. *Contemporary Way of the Cross: A Liturgical Journey along the Palestinian Via Dolorosa.* Jerusalem: Sabeel, 2008.

———. *The Jerusalem Sabeel Document.* Jerusalem: Sabeel, 2004.

Zaru, Jean. *Occupied with Nonviolence: A Palestinian Woman Speaks.* Ed. Diane L. Eck and Marla Schrader. Minneapolis: Augsburg Fortress, 2008

Theology of Land

Brueggemann, Walter. *The Land: Place as Gift, Promise, and Challenge in Biblical Theology.* 2nd ed. Minneapolis: Augsburg Fortress, 2002.

Burge, Gary M. *Jesus and the Land: The New Testament Challenge to 'Holy Land' Theology.* Grand Rapids: Baker Academic, 2010.

Davies, W. D. *The Gospel and the Land: Early Christianity and Jewish Territorial Doctrine.* Sheffield, UK: Sheffield Academic, 1994.

Habel, Norman C. *The Land is Mine: Six Biblical Land Ideologies.* Minneapolis: Fortress, 1995.

Smith-Christopher, Daniel. *A Biblical Theology of Exile.* Minneapolis: Augsburg Fortress, 2002.

Wilken, Robert Louis. *A Land Called Holy: Palestine in Christian History and Thought.* New Haven: Yale University Press, 1994.

CHAPTER THREE

Christian Zionism

Awad, Alex. "Christian Zionism: Their Theology, Our Nightmare." *MCC Peace Office Newsletter* 35/3 (July-September 2005) 2–3.

Clark, Victoria. *Allies for Armageddon: The Rise of Christian Zionism.* New Haven: Yale University Press, 2007.

Gorenberg, Gershom. *The End of Days: Fundamentalism and the Struggle for the Temple Mount.* Oxford: Oxford University Press, 2002.

Gunner, Göran, and Robert O. Smith, eds. *Comprehending Christian Zionism: Perspectives in Comparison.* Minneapolis: Fortress, 2014.

Leppäkari, Maria. *Apocalyptic Representations of Jerusalem.* Numen Book Series, Volume 111. Boston: Brill, 2006.

Lewis, Donald M. *The Origins of Christian Zionism: Lord Shaftesbury and Evangelical Support for a Jewish Homeland.* Cambridge: Cambridge University Press, 2014.

"Palestinian Church Leaders' Statement on Christian Zionism. 'We Stand for Justice: We Can Do No Other.'" *Holy Land Studies* 5 (November 2006) 211–13.

Smith, Robert O. *More Desired that Our Owne Salvation: The Roots of Christian Zionism.* Oxford: Oxford University Press, 2013.

Weber, Timothy. *On the Road to Armageddon: How Evangelicals Became Israel's Best Friend.* Grand Rapids: Baker Academic, 2004.

Revising Christian Theologies of Judaism

Awad, Alex. *Palestinian Memories: The Story of a Palestinian Mother and Her People.* Bethlehem: Bethlehem Bible College, 2008.

Boyarin, Daniel. *Border Lines: The Partition of Judaeo-Christianity.* Philadelphia: University of Pennsylvania Press, 2004.

———. *A Radical Jew: Paul and the Politics of Identity.* Berkeley: University of California Press, 1994.

Boys, Mary C. *Has God Only One Blessing? Judaism as a Source of Christian Self-Understanding.* Mahwah, NJ: Paulist, 2000.

Committee for Religious Relations with the Jews. *Notes on the Correct Way to Present Jews and Judaism in Preaching and Catechesis in the Roman Catholic Church.* Vatican, 1985. Available at http://

www.vatican.va/roman_curia/pontifical_councils/chrstuni/
relations-jews-docs/rc_pc_chrstuni_doc_19820306_jews-
judaism_en.html.

Diocesan Theological Commission of the Latin Patriarchate of Jerusalem. *Reflections on the Presence of the Church in the Holy Land.* December 3, 2003. Available at http://www.eohsj.net/LatinPatriarchTheologicalCommission.html.

Frymer-Kensky, Tikva, et al., eds. *Christianity in Jewish Terms.* Boulder, CO: Westview, 2000.

Joint Declaration of the 18th International Catholic-Jewish Liaison Meeting. Buenos Aires. July 5–8, 2004.

Ochs, Peter. *Another Reformation: Postliberal Christianity and the Jews.* Grand Rapids: Baker Academic, 2011.

Pope Paul VI. *Declaration on the Relation of the Church to Non-Christian Religions (Nostra Aetate).* Second Vatican Council. October 28, 1965. Available at http://www.vatican.va/archive/hist_councils/ii_vatican_council/documents/vat-ii_decl_19651028_nostra-aetate_en.html.

Sabbah, Michel. *Faithful Witness: Michel Sabbah on Peace and Reconciliation in the Holy Land.* Ed. Drew Christiansen, SJ, and Saliba Sarsar. Hyde Park, NY: New City, 2009.

———. *Reading the Bible Today in the Land of the Bible.* Fourth pastoral letter. Jerusalem: Latin Patriarchate, November 1993. Available at https://www.lpj.org/newsite2006/patriarch/pastoral-letters/1993/readingthebible_en.html.

Sherman, Franklin, ed. *Bridges: Documents of the Christian-Jewish Dialogue. Volume 1: The Road to Reconciliation.* Mahwah, NJ: Paulist, 2011.

Sherman, Franklin ed. *Bridges: Documents of the Christian-Jewish Dialogue. Volume 2: Building a New Relationship (1986–2013).* Mahwah, NY: Paulist, 2014.

World Council of Churches. *The Christian Approach to the Jews.* WCC Amsterdam Assembly. August 1, 1948. Available at https://www.oikoumene.org/en/resources/documents/assembly/1948-amsterdam/concerns-of-the-churches-the-christian-approach-to-the-jews.

———. *Resolution on Anti-Semitism.* WCC New Delhi Assembly. November 29, 1961. Available at http://www.jcrelations.net/A+Resolution+on+Antisemitism.1510.0.html?L=3.

CHAPTER FOUR

Azoulay, Ariella, and Adi Ophir. *The One State Condition: Occupation and Democracy in Israel/Palestine*. Stanford: Stanford University Press, 2012.

Darweish, Marwan and Andrew Rigby. *Popular Protest in Palestine: The History and Uncertain Future of Unarmed Resistance*. London: Pluto, 2015.

Ehrenreich, Ben. *The Way to the Spring: Life and Death in Palestine*. New York: Penguin, 2017.

Karmi, Ghada. *Return: A Memoir*. London: Verso, 2015.

Kairos Palestine. *A Moment of Truth: A Word of Faith, Hope, and Love from the Heart of Palestinian Suffering*. Jerusalem: Kairos Palestine, 2009.

Laor, Yitzhak. *The Myths of Liberal Zionism*. London: Verso, 2010.

Levine, Mark, and Matthias Mossberg, eds. *One Land, Two States: Israel and Palestine as Parallel States*. Berkeley, CA: University of California Press, 2014.

Nusseibeh, Sari. *What is a Palestinian State Worth?* Cambridge: Harvard University Press, 2011.

Said, Edward W. *Power, Politics, and Culture: Interviews with Edward W. Said*. New York: Vintage, 2002.

Shenhav, Yehouda. *Beyond the Two State Solution: A Jewish Political Essay*. New York: Polity, 2013.

Tilley, Virginia. *The One-State Solution: A Breakthrough for Peace in the Israeli-Palestinian Deadlock*. Ann Arbor: University of Michigan Press, 2005.

Weaver, Alain Epp. *Mapping Exile and Return: Palestinian Dispossession and a Political Theology for a Shared Future*. Minneapolis: Fortress, 2014.

Yiftachel, Oren. *Ethnocracy: Land and Identity Politics in Israel/Palestine*. Philadelphia: University of Pennsylvania Press, 2006.

Made in the USA
Middletown, DE
21 October 2018